The Dionysian Spirit

Published by
Mandrake of Oxford
PO Box 250
OXFORD
OX1 1AP (UK)

Devotional to Dionysos

"Appear, appear, whatsoever thy shape or name, O Mountain Bull, Snake of the Hundred Heads, Lion of the Burning Flame! O God, Beast, Mystery, come"

(Euripedes: The Bacchae)

EVOI EVOI DIONYSOS
EVOI DIONYSOS

DIONYSOS
DIONYSOS

EVOI DIONYSOS

Hear me Dionysos
Listen to me calling
Bring your wine and fire divine
Bring secret things to addle the mind
Hear me Dionysos

Come bellowing Dionysos
Clash cloven hooves of brass
Quake the ground for miles around
Gory horns and hooves that pound
Come bellowing Dionysos

Be beautiful Dionysos

You fey and girlish boy
Tempt me in ways I could never name
With silky skin and eyes aflame
Be beautiful Dionysos

Raise me Dionysos
Make me equal to yourself
Run through my veins, inflame my brains
Make me dance and scream your names
Raise me Dionysos

Liberate, Dionysos
Free this enslaved world
Those spiritless, joyless, mundane wrecks
Manacled to their office desks
Liberate, Dionysos

Be drunken Dionysos
You knackered, boozing lush
Be roaring, laughing, singing pissed
Horny as hell, Brahms and Liszt
Be drunken Dionysos

Destroy me Dionysos
Smash apart my shell
Crush my ego under your feet
Treat this body like so much meat
Destroy me Dionysos

Remake me Dionysos
Replace my faulty parts
Give me your heart, give me your eyes
Intoxicate me with your joys
Remake me Dionysos

Bring music Dionysos
Shrill flutes and heartbeat drums
Let Satyrs and Maenads dance and sing
While they rip apart the lion and the king
Bring music Dionysos

Be wild Dionysos
Wear ivy in your hair
Come as the leopard, the snake, the bull
Come as the thunder, come how you will
Be wild Dionysos

EVOI EVOI DIONYSOS
EVOI DIONYSOS

DIONYSOS
DIONYSOS
EVOI DIONYSOS

Seán Fitton
May 2009

Acknowledgements

It would have been impossible to write this book without the help, inspiration and patience of a great deal of people. Particular thanks go to my wife, Sara for putting up with my obsessions, my son, Emrys for teaching me how to deal with technology and my other children, Rowan and Phoebe for giving me other things to do.

Special mention must be made of Steve Ash (1961-2014) whose work in the Dionysian Underground has been my primary inspiration and whose historical information has been my primary source.

Thanks go also to the UK Pagan community as a whole, particularly the attendees of the Radcliffe Moot and other local moots who have allowed me to test my ideas on them.

Contents

Dedicated

To Sara
To the Dionysian Underground
To my Pagan friends
And to Dionysos Himself

Introduction

This book is about and in honour of Dionysos, the Greek god of wine and my own patron deity. It is also about more than that because Dionysos is rather more than simply a wine god. It is about something I have chosen to call *The Dionysian Spirit*.

It should be noted that this is not an academic book because I am not an academic, or even particularly well-educated, writer. Similarly, it is unlikely to be a book popular with a non-Pagan readership because I am a Pagan writer and thus must cannot help but write using language and terminology best comprehended by Pagans.

It is really a small guidebook by an ordinary Pagan for his fellow ordinary Pagans, intended to give them a taste of what Dionysos is, what he is all about: essentially what Dionysos is *for*. It is my fervent hope that people will use the ideas and information presented here as inspirations for their own researches and ideas.

The original version of this work started off as a moot topic for a Pagan discussion group. The idea was to introduce my friends to Dionysos, not simply as an entity in his own right, but also as a universal force in human culture; universal across the whole of the time-space continuum. He is the voice that the mystic can hear, the shadow that exists where there is light, the Yin that gives balance to the Yang,

The Dionysian Spirit is the spirit of nonconformity, revolution and, to a certain extent, chaos which has informed change, evolution and revolution in human society even before Dionysos himself was named. It is the spirit which moves the shaman into a realm beyond the confines of his body, which gives ecstasy to the Christian mystic, which brings the artist and composer to create their most heart-rending works and the anarchist to the edge of throwing the petrol bomb.

It is my intention throughout this book to show how the spirit of Dionysos, in some forms the oldest of the gods and in others the youngest, has brought the human race to its greatest peaks and lowest troughs. In many cases the notions of peaks and troughs are entirely a matter of opinion, in many others they may even be the selfsame thing. I shall leave that to the reader to decide. The facts remain, though, that he is still doing it and that we still need him to carry on, *now more than ever.*

Since this book is being written by a good Pagan boy for other good Pagan boys and girls (amongst others), we will start off in a good and traditional Pagan way, with a visualization exercise or *Pathworking.* If you have never done a Pathworking before, the usual method is to sit relaxed in a darkened room while somebody else tells a story. You would then use the power of your imagination to visualise yourself in that story.

You could do that, if you wanted to. You could even tape yourself reading it and then use that for the exercise. In reality, for this particular pathworking it will be sufficient to picture the events in your mind's eye while you read. The purpose of the exercise is to give you a taste of the effect the Dionysian cult had on Ancient Greece.

So … Are you sitting comfortably? Then we'll begin.

The Visualization

See with the eye of your imagination. Cast your mind backwards 3,000 years and south-eastwards (from Britain anyway) about 1,600 miles to Athens, in the Classical period.

You are a respectable and successful middle-aged gentleman of about 35 years old. You have a beard, a balding head and a paunch making a bulge in your toga. You are sitting with other respectable middle-aged gentlemen talking about respectable middle-aged things.

The *extremely* respectable villa on the outskirts of Athens in which you relax on this lovely warm evening isn't yours; it belongs to a good friend, a slave trader.

Other good friends are there too: an architect, a sophist, a mathematician, an olive grower. The talk is on sensible and important, manly subjects such as barley exports, relations with Sparta, the heroes of the latest games and the ethics of Plato's Republic. The wine is almost perfectly warmed and watered, and is being served by a rather attractive young man, a protégé of your slave-trader friend.

All's right with the world. The Gods are on Olympus, keeping out of mankind's affairs; the slaves are sweeping the streets and shifting the night soil and - most importantly - the women are safely locked away at home doing whatever it is that women do. Embroidery or babies or some such nonsense.

As the light is fading you notice a spark of orange on the hillside about half a mile away, and you can hear faint pipe music.

It appears that someone has lit a fire in the olive fields! Of course, you and your friends are just the upright citizens to investigate.

When you reach the grove an absolutely disgraceful sight greets you. From behind a bush you can see people dancing around an open fire. Their music isn't anything like the proper and approved cithara music of the squares and temples. It has high, wailing reed-pipes and heavy, pounding drums.

The people are even worse. There are peasants here, farmers and labourers. There are slaves here too - in fact it's possible that you recognise a couple of them.

Worst of all there are women here. Women outdoors, at night, without chaperones! Lots of women, in fact. With loose hair, sweaty faces and wild expressions. They are dancing madly with no thought to the fact that their clothes falling off. Not just young and single women either, there are middle-aged and older women here too.

In fact, that one there . . . could it be . . . oh, shame of shames . . .

It's your mother!

If you are performing the Pathworking properly, now is the time to come back to the normal world. Slowly and gently, please.

It seems that your imaginary Ancient Greek mother has met, danced and drank with Dionysos. The first section of the book will allow you to meet him too. Don't forget to bring a bottle!

The Myths of Dionysos

Ancient Greece

The myths and stories of Dionysos as we know them best come to us from Ancient Greece. It is important to remember that the people who told, heard and wrote those tales were the product of a very different culture than ourselves in the modern Western world. Thus, their understanding of and reactions to stories would be rather different from our own. The concepts of worship, at least as far as Dionysos is concerned, were also rather different, and had a radical and sometimes shocking effect on Ancient Greek society as a whole.

When looking at a culture's mythology it seems, therefore, a good idea to examine it in context.

When we mention Ancient Greece most of us think of long-bearded philosophers in togas. To be fair they did exist, as can be attested from the statues, but they were very much in the minority. It is also said that the Greeks gave us democracy, which again is true, but not the sort of democracy which we are used to.

One thing which you would hardly ever see on the streets of an ancient Greek city was a woman. Ancient Greece has been jokingly described as a phallocracy. That's possibly a little facetious, but not actually inaccurate. The only people with any political power whatsoever were mature, free, wealthy men of good social standing.

Notwithstanding statues of goddesses, early Greek culture was entirely male-dominated. Women in this culture were often of lower value than slaves, being considered as little more than a necessity for breeding. All commerce (with the exception of prostitution) was entirely male-controlled, as were art, music, warfare, politics and every other area of public life.

It would be fairer to say that it was not simply women who were considered inferior, it was the whole perception of femininity. Qualities considered feminine, such as powerful or uncontrolled emotionality and a love of luxury and home comforts, were very much down-played in Ancient Greek society in favour of "masculine" virtues like correct behaviour, rationality and nationalism. Even in Sparta, where women and men had a relatively equal position in society, the women could only hold their position by being "masculine", by those terms.

Ancient Greek religion was staid and controlled, also masculine in fact. Priesthoods were employed to interpret the will of the godsand the gods themselves were considered as distant and separate from human beings. By way of an example, if you wished to petition the god, Ares you would first go to the Temple of Ares and tell the priest what you want. The priest would then tell you the price, usually in terms of what sacrifice was required. You would then make the appropriate sacrifice and the priest would petition Ares on your behalf, giving you the answer later should you require one. As one would expect, sacrifices were expensive and well beyond the means of working peasants.

By the time of Plato and Aristotle, philosophers had even come to the point of questioning whether the gods existed at all.

As I stated above, the virtues of Ancient Greek life were "masculine" virtues: strength, emotional self-control, warlike attitudes, logical thought, order and obedience. The feminine virtues, such as nurturing or deep emotionality, were regarded as unworthy and things to be suppressed. Homosexuality, on the other hand was not.

One of the strangest of our modern concepts is the equation of male homosexuality and effeminacy. There is no good reason for this because it is perfectly possible to be macho and homosexual just as it is perfectly possible to effeminate and heterosexual, yet we still do it. Popular culture regularly potrays gay men as "limp-wristed" and camp, and slightly effeminate boys are often mercilessly bullied at school for being "puffs"

In the early Greek city states almost the opposite applied. Effeminacy was abhorred, and indeed the ultimate expression of beauty was considered to be the body of the healthy young male athlete. Homosexuality was not simply allowed; it was admired, respected and even required – but only in certain circumstances.

In the normal course of an upwardly-mobile young man's life it was expected that he be "patroned" by a successful or aristocratic older man. The boy was called the *eromenos* and his patron the *erastes*. The older man would enter into a relationship with the boy, at about the age of twelve, in which he would educate him in the ways of the world. He would help him in his career, attempt to find him a worthy marriage and often have sex with him, anally and as the dominant partner. The older man was considered unusual but excusable if he fell in love with the boy. He gave the boy advantages in life and the boy gave him pleasure. The boy was not normally expected to enjoy the relationship.

In his turn, and after some years, the boy was supposed to carry on the tradition with the adoption of a young lover of his own. This system was not only a social expectation, it was actually a legal requirement in some states at certain times.[1]

Similarly the armies, particularly in Sparta, encouraged homosexual relationships amongst its soldiers as a means of engendering loyalty within the ranks. Two lovers fighting side-by-side were considered an awesome and terrifying prospect. It is no great surprise to find that the Hollywood film industry has ignored this aspect of Classical culture, so far!

Into this testosterone-flooded arena, then, stepped a rather girly young demigod, like a flamboyant, eyeliner-wearing Emo kid into a Skinhead pub. Sparks did, indeed, fly.

To understand what happened, we need to look firstly at the actual myths themselves concerning Dionysos, and then we will be able to see how his worship affected the ancient world.

The Birth of Dionysos

According to the most popular story, Dionysos is[1] born in Thrace. Thrace is an area above the north-eastern end of the Aegean Sea, equating in modern geography roughly to the borderlands between far north-eastern Greece, north-western Turkey and southern Bulgaria. The Thracians were infamous in Classical thought for their reputed drunkenness.

An alternative version places his birth in Lydia, a region of mid-western Turkey, whose inhabitants were noted for their voluptuousness and effeminacy. It is considered by many scholars that Dionysos' other name, Bacchus may derive from Backhos, a Lydian name.

These are the first instances of the confusion between the myths and the perception of Dionysos as a god: the fact that he is not really Greek. By our standards he is Turkish, but the most important point from the Ancient Greek viewpoint was that he is foreign, alien, an imported god who causes trouble because he does not fit in.

The story begins, as many do, with the chief god of the Olympian pantheon, Zeus, and his dalliance with a mortal woman called Semele. Zeus dallies with quite a few mortal women, producing many of the demigods and heroes of Greek mythology. Semele is a princess, the daughter of King Cadmus of Thebes and the aunt of the later and more famous king of Thebes, Pentheus. Interestingly, as Thebes is in southern Greece, this does not equate with Dionysos' birth in Turkey, but it can be noted that Semele is considered by many experts not to be a Greek name.

In another version, Semele is a priestess of Zeus. It is, of course, eminently possible that she is both.

When Semele is six months pregnant Zeus' jealous wife, the goddess Hera, appears to her in the guise of an ancient nurse named Beroë. Using her wiles and intelligence Beroë lays a seed of doubt into the mind of Semele and persuades her to question Zeus divinity.

Semele does this by asking him to reveal himself in his full glory as a thunderbolt.

Zeus is now stuck with a dreadful quandary. He has promised to deny Semele nothing, but at the same time he knows that the sight of his true self will kill Semele outright. Unfortunately she insists and is burned, as expected, to a cinder.

Just at the moment of her death the fleet messenger of the gods, Hermes, flies in and rescues the unborn child from Semele's womb. Lacking a better place he then sews the foetus into Zeus' thigh. Dionysos completes his gestation in this rather unsuitable and makeshift womb, and consequently becomes known as the "twice-born".

Here, then, is another of those confusing Dionysian contradictions. Dionysos isn't really a god after all – he is *half-human*. This is such a remarkably important point it is difficult to stress it enough. Dionysos is not a god, or a human, he is halfway between. I have already mentioned the way Ancient Greek religion worked and Dionysos stands in direct opposition to that method. He is a direct bridge between the gods and humanity.

Dionysos' Childhood

The newly-born Dionysos is, of course, half divine and thus able to walk, talk and play at birth. He is a beautiful but also odd-looking child, being blessed with a small pair of bull's horns.

As is the way of young children he heads straight for his father's throne and starts playing with the thunderbolts. Because of his divinity they cannot do him any harm, and they are certainly more interesting than his toys which are described as[1]: a ball, a top, some dice, some golden apples, a bit of wool, a bull-roarer and a mirror. These seven items have a mythological significance beyond the scope of this piece, but if any reader wishes to investigate further I would recommend starting with the works of Robert Graves.

Hera is, of course, still jealous and plotting the child's destruction. With this in mind she sends in a group of her Titans while he is playing, their faces whitened with chalk, intending for them to kill him with their knives. Young Dionysos spots them and runs for it. There follows a chase in which Dionysos, in common with many other mythological and magical heroes, changes into several shapes in order to evade his pursuers. These seven shapes are[2]: Zeus, Cronos (Zeus' father), a young man, a lion, a horse, a serpent and bull. The Titans finally catch up with their quarry and kill him, cutting his body into seven pieces. It is said that the first pomegranate tree springs from his blood.

The Titans then cook and eat all the pieces of the body except one, the heart. This is rescued by Rhea, the wife of Cronos and Dionysos' divine grandmother, an earth-mother goddess who resides in Phrygia (north-west Turkey). She uses the heart to recreate the infant Dionysos and, in order to keep him safe from Hera, gives him to the Nysaean Nymphs to nurse, disguised as a kid (ie. young goat).

The Nymphs, for their part, disguise Dionysos and bring him up as a girl. In reward for their aid, Zeus places them in the heavens where they become the star cluster known as the Hyades.

Early Life

There is not a great deal written about Dionysos' life as a youth[1] because he spends the majority of it sequestered with the Nysaean Nymphs. Even so, there are a few important pointers to his nature hidden away. Importantly amongst these is the fact that, despite his effeminacy, Zeus decides to recognize his son when he comes of age. But he does not take him up to Olympus to live among the other gods. Instead he ordains that Dionysos must live among men and share their suffering.

It is said that he discovers, or possibly creates, the grape vine and viticulture at this time. Thus he is given the wonderful epithet of *The Deliverer*, because his gift of wine delivers men from their cares.

He often appears as a goat or - much more often - a bull, rather than in his more usual form of an effeminate young man, and acquires a large group of followers and fellow travellers, who become known as the Thiasos[2], Bacchae or Bacchantes. Amongst these are Satyrs (sexually voracious goat-men) and Silenes (similar but with horse attributes). Most importantly, there are Maenads (*pron.* Mee-nad). Maenads are wild, powerful, lustful and thoroughly drunken, human women.

Hera again steps in at this point for one last try, and drives our young hero insane. She then leaves him to wander the earth. It is fairly certain that this theme will be familiar to a great many readers of mythology, for instance the story of Merlin's madness in the *Vita Merlini* and possibly even the biblical story of Jesus in the wilderness

In Phrygia he chances upon his grandmother, Rhea again. She restores his sanity and *teaches him her rites*. After that he sets off with his entourage across Asia Minor and as far as India, spreading the worship of the ancient Earth Mother and teaching viticulture as he goes.

Here again is another Dionysian difficulty: the worship of Dionysos is really not the worship of Dionysos at all, it is the worship of Rhea. It is this author's opinion that there is every possibility that the Dionysian cult of Ancient Greece was a direct descendant of the rites of much older middle-Eastern matriarchal hunter-gatherer societies. It is very difficult to provide evidence for such a position, but there are close correlations in such societies as the Minangkabau of West Sumatra and the Mosuo people who live close to Lugu Lake in China.

The Bacchae

The most famous story of Dionysos is, undoubtedly *The Bacchae*[1], which was written as a play by Euripides and performed posthumously at the Dionysia in Athens in 405 BC. The Dionysia was a festival of theatre in honour of Dionysos.

In *The Bacchae*, Dionysos brings his rites into the Greek city of Thebes, which is ruled by the young king, Pentheus. Pentheus is, in fact, Dionysos' cousin. Pentheus mother is Agave, one of the four daughters of Cadmus and Harmonia, the others being Semele (now deceased), Autonoe and Ino. The family refuse to accept him as the son of Zeus, instead preferring to believe that Semele lied about the identity of her baby's father. Worse than that, Pentheus takes the unprecedented step of banning Dionysian rites on Theban land.

Appearing in the city disguised as his own high priest, Dionysos casts a spell over the Theban women, driving them to his rites. Even the old men become enamoured of his festivities, and attempt to go to the Bacchanale disguised as women. Pentheus prevents the men from attending and, as he refuses to tell all of what goes on, Pentheus has the young god imprisoned. Obviously such an insult could not go unpunished, so Dionysos causes environmental havoc in the city.

Later, Pentheus hears stories of the wonders performed by the Maenads in their ecstasies from a "stranger" (the reader is invited to guess who that might be!) and decides that he must see for himself. The stranger persuades Pentheus that he must look like a Maenad in order to get into the rituals and, after befuddling his mind, dresses him in women's clothes and parades him through the streets on the way to the rites.

He then persuades Pentheus to climb a pine tree in order to get a good view. It is at this point that Dionysos reveals himself and points Pentheus out to the Bacchae. They drag him out of the tree and tear him to pieces with their bare hands, hallucinating that he is a lion. Agave herself rips off his head and carries it back into Thebes.

The shock, when the hallucination finally wears off, destroys the Theban royal family. Agave and her sisters are sent into exile and Dionysos turns Cadmus and Harmonia into snakes. The only person to get off scot-free is Tiresias, a prophet and friend to Cadmus, who had warned Pentheus of the foolishness of not accepting Dionysos.

The moral of the story, of course, is not to insult the gods. They will get you back and they have a grim sense of humour. There also the possibility that Euripedes wrote the story as a kind-of anti-Bacchanale propaganda, although that seems unlikely. By the time of the play's first performance, Dionysos was already firmly established as the god of the Theatre

Lycurgus

Another story tells how similar thing to Pentheus' fate also happens to king Lycurgus of Thrace, who has all Dionysos' followers imprisoned. Dionysos sends a drought, causing revolt amongst the king's subjects. He then makes the king insane and causes him to hallucinate that his own son is a patch of ivy with the result that Lycurgus chops him up with an axe. An oracle states that the drought would remain in place until Lycurgus' death, so the people have him drawn and quartered.

Other Tales

Dionysos also appears in a number of other myths, although normally in a non-starring role. The most well known of these is the story of King Midas.

In brief, Midas of Phrygia finds a drunken creature asleep in his rose garden one morning. The creature turns out to be Silenos, the tutor and foster father of Dionysos. Midas entertains him royally and escorts him back to the Bacchantes. In reward for this fine treatment Dionysos offers him any wish he may choose. As all schoolchildren know (or ought to!), Midas asks that everything he touches turn to gold.

The result of such a stupid wish is fairly plain and, eventually, Midas returns to Dionysos to beg for a cure. He is told to bathe in the fountain-head of the River Pactolus, which turns the sand to gold.

Love and Sex

Dionysos has a number of sexual adventures, the most important of which is with his wife, Ariadne. Dionysos meets the Cretan princess when she is mysteriously stranded on the island of Naxos by Theseus after his adventure with the Minotaur. He gives her a crown of gold and gems, and when she dies he places it in the heavens as the constellation, Corona Borealis. Between them they are considered to be the parents of a number of Aegean tribes and mythological figures including Oenopion, the king of Chios and a personification of wine.

His other relationships include a dalliance with Aphrodite, who bears the ithyphallic god, Priapus and also (in one version) with Althea, through whom he becomes the father of Hercules' wife Deianeira. He is considered, in some versions, to have a relationship with the night-goddess, Nyx who bears Phthonus, and Ovid makes him the father of Acis, the spirit of the River Acis in Sicily.

One of the major problems we have when we read mythology is the attitude of the people who wrote it. We should be thankful to our academic and intellectual Victorian forbears who discovered, translated and published the majority of the world's mythology which is available to us. Unfortunately, hypocritical Victorian morality was as strong as the Victorian urge to rediscover the human "Golden Age" and the result was that many of the myths were made morally edifying. It was perfectly accepted practise for morally questionable events in myths, such as homosexual relations, to be edited out so as not to corrupt women and the lower orders who may happen upon them. This was normal behaviour, but has had the knock-on effect that we are still reading those versions of the myths now, and it is only in the last ten to twenty years that such editing has been rediscovered and put back. Personally, I am reminded of the judge who made his opinion plain about D.H. Lawrence's most famous book, *Lady Chatterly's Lover*, with the question, "Would you let your wife or servants read this book?"

Dionysos does, in fact, have sexual relationships with several male deities and mythological characters, one of whom may even be Apollo[1]. The first of these lovers is Hyacinthus, although frankly just about every god on Olympus has a little fun with Hyacinthus at some point. He is a very popular young man. Another is the satyr youth, Ampelos. Sadly, Ampelos is killed riding a bull which has been stung by Ate, a personification of folly. The fates grant Ampelos a second life as a vine, from which Dionysos squeezes the first wine.

Finally, there are myths where Dionysos rescues Ariadne and Semele from the underworld, and a lover is also involved here. The guide into Hades is the old shepherd, Prosymnus, who asks to be

Dionysos' lover as the price of his services. Unfortunately, Prosymnus dies before his return, so (according to certain sources[2]) he honours the debt by making and ritually using a false penis of fig or olive wood, by placing it on Prosymnus' grave and sitting on it. This is the source of the wooden phallus carried in Dionysian processions.

Semele is taken to Olympus and given the magnificent new name, Thyone, which translates as Raging Queen.

As a complete end to Dionysos' story, Dionysos is taken to Olympus by Zeus and accepted as one of the Twelve Olympians of the Greek pantheon. In doing so he displaces the goddess, Hestia who is actually rather glad of the rest from all the politics, in-fighting and back-bighting of life on Olympus.

It should, of course, come as no surprise that Greek mythology would include homosexual relationships although, considering the nature of Ancient Greek society, homosexuality between social equals was less common. It is also no surprise that the British and American collectors of the Victorian period and early twentieth century would judiciously edit them out wherever possible. The fascinating concept, and one which will become incredibly important a little later, is that one love-interest is Apollo.

Behind the Myths

As with all mythology, the stories of Dionysos are rather more than simply fireside tales. They contain both literal histories and psycho-spiritual truths hidden in an encoded form. Combined with known historical fact, the study of the myths can lead to some wonderful insights.

Firstly we know from historians that the worship of Dionysos was unknown in Greece before the 7th Century BCE, and that he became prominent in a variety of Earth Mother cults[1] such as the Eleusinian Mysteries of Demeter. This naturally implies, and is shown by his birth-stories, that Dionysian worship already existed outside Greece and had spread. The places to which he is most strongly connected are Thrace, Lydia and Phrygia.

The peoples of Thrace were considered as "rude tribes" and notorious drunkards by the more urbane Greeks. There was a loose confederation of rural tribes residing in various hill forts and farmsteads, but without any large-scale social cohesion or urbanization until a great deal of Greek influence had been assimilated. They were also considered a belligerent, aggressive people and often employed as mercenaries. In many respects the Thracians of the 7th to 4th centuries BCE could be considered as culturally very similar to the later Celts. The Greeks also considered them to be the inventors of tattooing which, by the time of Plato, was a practise limited to slaves.

Dionysos' other birthplace was thought to be Lydia, in the area around Mt Sipylus west of what is now Izmir. Lydians were thought of as voluptuous and effeminate, which was most likely a cultural prejudice on the part of the Greeks - much as the modern western man's opinion of, for instance, traditional Nigerian dress. I have already mentioned the Ancient Greek attitude to male effeminacy.

The third place of importance, Phrygia, is very obviously the centre of a powerful Earth Mother cult, the cult of a goddess who the Romans referred to as Cybele. The Phrygians originally came from Thrace[2] and so shared in the Thracian reputation. In Greek and also in much later art in Europe the Phrygian cap, a soft conical red hat, came to represent the spirit of non-conformism and liberty. It can be seen in many paintings of events, both real and imagined, concerning the French Revolution.

Classical period Greek music was played in a variety of styles called modes, two of which are known as the Lydian and the Phrygian, named after the tribes of those areas. The Phrygian mode was considered the most warlike. Plato disapproved of the use of the Lydian mode[3] (amongst others) because of its tendency to induce softness and sloth.

The sewing of the almost-born Dionysos into his father's thigh seems strange and arbitrary at first but could be a much corrupted version of the concept of the sacred thigh[4], whereby the thigh of an important person is damaged thus raising the heel off the ground. It is interesting to note that actors wore high-heeled shoes called *cothurnus* in honour of Dionysos, which raised the heel off the ground and gave the wearer a mincing gait[5].

A simpler explanation, though, might be that of a patriarchal claim to parenthood by emulating the birth process. It can be said that the thigh is a euphemism for the male genitalia and there is a biblical example in Genesis 24:2 where Abraham's servant makes a vow by placing his hand under his master's thigh. It is quite possible that the traditional prayer position of kneeling with hands folded comes from a position of servitude with the hands "under the thigh" (ie touching the genitals, being the seat of masculine power) of the seated or standing superior. This would place the superior in an almost paternal position and there is a theory that the practise could be related to some very ancient middle-Eastern adoption rituals.

The hatred of Hera seems to have much to do with the supplanting of one Earth Mother's rituals (Rhea) for another, and her connection with the Titans implies an antiquity which would make Hera older than the Olympian pantheon. Obviously this does not sit well with the mythology as it stands, Hera being the daughter of Rhea and the older sister, as well as the wife, of Zeus. It would suggest that the cult of Hera was absorbed by the Olympians, modernizing her worship, and that the cult of Rhea (Demeter/Cybele) and Dionysos would become a threat because it would be a return to an older way of belief.

The shape-changing element is fascinating in its similarity to many other mythologies, particularly the transformation chase of Gwion Bach as he runs away from the Earth Mother/witch figure of Cerridwen[6]. Many Pagan writers and scholars consider these shapeshifting activities as poetic descriptions of shamanic initiation whereby the shaman would invoke the spirits of local animals and the tribe's ancestors. It also shows that Dionysos has an animal side and avatars such as the bull.

A similar comment could equally be made about the sacrificial elements in the story. The tearing or cutting apart followed by being rebuilt by a deity recalls many of the worldwide shamanic traditions of death and rebirth initiations. At the same time many writers[7] consider the sacrificial death of the young god as a symbolic representation of the annual death of the king of a tribe, or his replacement, which they considered to have been prevalent in Europe some time before the Bronze Age. Either of these theories is valid, and it is possible that both are equally true, being closely related concepts.

There are a number of annually dying and rebirthing gods in the western pantheons, among them Adonis, Baldur, Osiris and Attis. Most of them are related to solar cults and the farming of cereals such as wheat and barley and, like Gwion Bach/Taliesin, are sacrificed at the hand or control of a female character. Although Dionysos has lost any strong solar associations he may have had, and his plant is only pruned rather than completely chopped down, he still appears to be of that archetypal pattern. It is possibly the loss of solar associations which make Dionysos stand out from his peers.

The insanity of Dionysos and his wandering the earth are also fairly common themes in mythology, but not usually in the myths of gods. It is normally demigods or great heroes, for instance Merlin[8,] who are subject to such tribulations. Again, this smacks of shamanism as both an initiation process and also the "insanity" of difference from normal life found among those who practise shamanic techniques.

The fact of Zeus ordaining that Dionysos spend his life among humans and sharing in their suffering immediately shows how alien he is to the Olympian pantheon. The gods of the ancient Greeks were distant and transcendent. They occasionally affected humans in both good and bad ways and they could be contacted via the offices of the various priesthoods, but they mostly stayed on Mount Olympus and out of human affairs. The idea of a god being here, now, and willing to join with his followers in the most intimate ways was completely radical and all but unthinkable to an educated classical-period Athenian. Most of Dionysos' disciples were of low class: farmers, slaves and, most importantly at the time, women. There was little use for organized and formalized state religion amongst these people – what they needed was escape from their bondage, which is what the new young god gave them.

The stories of Pentheus and Lycurgus have a feeling of being later and more well organized than the other tales, but still fit the pattern of the dead and resurrected king. In this case the sacrifice is a substitute for the real thing, but a sacrifice nonetheless.

Dionysos to Jesus via Orpheus

We know from the histories and the plays of Greek writers and more modern scholars that Dionysos was known as a god of wine and drunkenness. He received many epithets such as *Bromios* (thunderer), *Lusios* (loosener) and *Lyiasos* (deliverer). His followers were mostly poor, uneducated, rural people with very little institutionalized religion but a close connection to the natural world through farming and hunting/gathering.

The Maenads were pictured as wild women running and dancing

with torches and *thyrsus*, a type of wand or staff made of a fennel stalk topped with a pine cone and wound round with ivy. He was visualized as a goat or (more usually) a bull and his processions would include the carrying of a giant phallus. He was served by lecherous, ithyphallic and animalistic satyrs and silenes

To his followers, then, he would represent the power of wine (or one of many other intoxicants) to release inhibitions and bring joy and a ritual outlet of freedom - the *Bacchanale* (from his other name, *Bacchos*) - into a fairly basic and often miserable existence. At the same time he could also represent the social and beneficial effects of wine. By way of an example, the self-sufficiency writer, John Seymour told a story in his book, *The Complete book of Self-Sufficiency* of how he was stationed, during World War II with the King's African Rifles. They had a company brewer who could make an alcoholic beverage out of any farinaceous grain. As Seymour said, "It was rough stuff, but it kept us sane!"

According to some writers, the original intoxicant may have been the red and white "fairy mushroom", Fly Agaric (*Amanita Muscaria*)[1], which gives enormous physical strength, erotic power, delirious visions and, apparently, the gift of prophecy.

Dionysos has a secondary role as a god of trees, particularly fruit trees. He was often depicted by the use of an upright post draped with a mantle and a bearded mask, and with leafy branches protruding. In this aspect his sacred trees are the pine (see what happens to Pentheus in *The Bacchae*), apple, fig, ivy and, of course, the grape vine.

He does also have certain commonalities with corn gods in that his cradle is supposed to have been a winnowing fan and he is said to have invented ploughing with a bull.

One of the most interesting, but seemingly unrelated, aspects of Dionysos is his place as the god of theatre. According to Aristotle, Tragedy (a form of Greek theatre along with Comedy and Farce) was a development of Dionysian ritual. The word "trageodia" means "goat-song", possibly referring to the costumes worn by singers and actors playing satyrs in honour of Dionysos. Early ritual would have consisted of a spiritual surrender involving chants and rudimentary dramatic action, much in the style of a tribal shaman giving life to a spirit animal. Full-fledged acting is, therefore, an evolved form of this ritual.

The Dionysia was a theatrical festival held during December (in rural areas) or March (in Athens itself) in which plays and processions were performed and which were times for the suspension of normal rules of behaviour, much like the later Roman Saturnalia or the mediaeval Feast of Fools. As the name suggests they were held in honour of Dionysos, and were likely to have been introduced around the 6th century BCE. The swaying walk of the *cothurnus*-wearing actors is thought to be a deliberate and erotic flaunting of one's sexual charms, and an actor was one of the few men in Ancient Greek society for whom being effeminate was considered acceptable. Even today actors are considered "luvvies" but interestingly, it is now common in the western world for women to wear unusually high heels, for exactly the same reason as the ancient actors.

Dionysos birthday is officially the 6th of January, but his death and rebirth were celebrated at the Lenaea Winter Solstice ritual in Athens, also known as the festival of the wild women. He is connected to two other important Greek festivals: *Anthesterion* and *Mykosterion*, respectively flower- and mushroom-uprising.

Eventually, the worship of Dionysos became accepted and institutionalized, which is the "real world" equivalent of his acceptance onto Olympus. It became legally recognized, and so legally controlled, in Corinth, Delphi, Sparta and Athens by the 5th century BCE.

The most important difference between Dionysos and the other gods of Greece was his immanence. His rituals were orgiastic and usually involved the physical sacrifice of an animal (possibly, but very rarely, a person) which was then torn apart and eaten. The point here is that it was not the animal that was killed, but the god in the form of that animal and the eating of its flesh was to truly take the god into oneself and join with him. In other words this was a form of invocation whereby the worshipper would literally become one with Dionysos. In the controlled and rule-laden world of ancient Greece, Dionysos provided two things that no other god could: *ecstasy* and *enthusiasm*.

These words have become rather weakened over time but they are much more powerful in their original senses. Enthusiasm comes from *en* and *theos*. Rather than the insipid modern meaning of a strong interest in something, it literally means to take a god within oneself. In other words to have the spirit of a god within is to become one with that god, to *be* that god.

The other of Dionysos' gifts is ecstasy or, in Greek, *ekstasis*. Literally, *ekstasis* is to "stand outside" of oneself. This is to completely go beyond one's limitations in any and every way, to acquire complete freedom, to become something other than human. Bertrand Russell[2] explained beautifully that the cult of Dionysos allowed the newly civilized people of Ancient Greece to: "*Recover an intensity of feeling (ie. passion) which prudence had destroyed; he finds the world full of delight and beauty, and his imagination is suddenly liberated from the prison of every-day occupations*"

Fortunately, it is not necessary to go into the mythology of Orpheus in any great depth here. His stories are almost as complex and confusing as those of Dionysos. A brief outline of the best known versions goes like this:

Orpheus is the son of a Thracian king (or the god Apollo) and the muse Calliope. He is raised by his mother and her eight sisters on Mount Parnassus where he meets Apollo who teaches him to play the lyre. His mother also teaches him how to write songs and sing them.

He is considered the greatest musician in the world with the power to charm animals and people, move trees and rocks to dancing, and divert the course of rivers. He becomes a harrower of hell when he attempts to rescue his wife, Eurydice from Hades. He is also a member of Jason's crew on the Argo.

Orpheus death is particularly significant in that he is torn apart by Maenads who throw his head into the River Hebron. The head remains alive and singing for some time afterwards.

It can be seen that there are many correlations between Orpheus and Dionysos: the Thracian birth, the semi-divine status and the upbringing entirely by women in his early life, and the death by being torn apart. He is even thought in many versions to be a follower of Dionysos. In mythical terms "follower" or "son" can often mean a later version. He certainly shares with Dionysos the tendency to emotionalism and identification with the natural and feminine, as opposed to the city-based and man-made.

Orpheus death is open to many, and often conflicting, interpretations. The most common is that Orpheus denied the worship of all the gods except Apollo and preached homosexual love and that Dionysos had him killed in revenge. This seems quite unlikely and my own opinion is that he was a substitute sacrifice, taking the place of Dionysos himself and being torn apart by maenads as a bull would be as part of a sacrificial ceremony. This would explain why his head, still singing after floating all the way to Lesbos, was placed in a cave at Antissa which was sacred to Dionysos.

Orphism itself became a religion around the 5th century BCE. The Orphics worshipped Dionysos/Bacchos by the name, Zagreus, who they considered to be the sun by day and fire by night. They also worshipped Persephone/Kore who they regarded as Zagreus' mother. The Orphics respected powerful emotion rather than he "good behaviour" expected in normal life, and were highly feminist, allowing equal status to both women and men. They also looked to personal revelation as their ultimate source of authority. The main difference between Orphism and Bacchism was that the former was far more ascetic in basis and regarded mental intoxication as above and beyond physical intoxication[3].

According to Robert Graves[4], the major Orphic ritual involved the killing of Zagreus in the form of a kid and the boiling of the flesh in its mother's milk. The meat would then be eaten to absorb and become one with Zagreus. Graves states that from this comes the origin of the Jewish ban on eating milk and meat together[5].

The spiritualized Bacchism of the Orphics spread from its original home in Attica across southern Italy and Sicily, greatly influencing religious thought as it went. Pythagorean philosophy is considered to be a development of Orphism. Most importantly and radically, the Orphics created the first "churches", religious communities to which anybody could be admitted by initiation, regardless of any distinctions of race, class or sex[6].

The early churches of Christianity (before Constantine) followed the Orphic pattern and appealed strongly to the poor and downtrodden. According to many, Jesus was connected to an ascetic Jewish cult known as the Essenes, who developed the majority of their doctrine from Pythagorean philosophy and, therefore, Orphism[7]. Whether this is true or not, there are remarkable similarities in evidence which are highly likely to have evolved from previous doctrines. One of these is that, especially considering that there was no written scripture until more than sixty years after Jesus' death, spiritual surrender was considered paramount. Knowledge and correct behaviour were not considered as particularly important in comparison.

The most striking similarity comes in the form of the sacrament or Holy Communion. This is, of course, a substitute sacrifice ritual where bread and wine are used to replace flesh and blood, just as the flesh and blood of a bull could be used to replace the flesh and blood of Dionysos himself. Jesus is quoted as saying *"Take this bread and eat it; this is my body"*[8]. In other words the Christians were, and still are, becoming one with their sacrificed and reborn demigod by eating and drinking his body and blood.

For many early Christians this ritual could bring such *ecstasy* and *enthusiasm* that they would suffer torture, degradation and gruesome death for their faith rather than subject themselves to any kind of distant religious authority such as that of Imperial Rome.

The Spirit of Dionysos as a Paradigm

Am I saying here that Jesus was really Pythagoras, who was really Orpheus, who was really Dionysos? No, I am not. But what I am saying is that the Spirit of Dionysos, that spirit of life in all its chaotic, anti-establishment glory, has run through the teachings of these gods, demigods, philosophers and musicians over several millennia, if not since human beings first noticed and established an understanding and concept of gods..

Earlier I mentioned a love affair between Dionysos and Apollo. This is significant in terms of paradigms because of the natural opposition and balance of the two gods. Dionysos is a god of nature, life, of liberation and intoxication. He represents all those aspects that are wild and passionate in our human nature. He personifies spiritual surrender and emotional release, enthusiasm, ecstasy and primal reality. His arts are dynamic and life-affirming, such as music, theatre and dance.

Apollo is a god of order, rationality civilization. He represents balance and moderation, and all those qualities that are idealized and static. His art is made of permanent, unchanging things like sculpture, painting and architecture.

Dionysos is Yin to Apollo's Yang, the Id to his Ego, the drunk to his sober. The two must be kept in balance. A society unbalanced in favour of Apollo becomes totalitarian, monolithic and intolerant; one overly biased towards Dionysos becomes decadent, debauched and self-destructive. Exactly the same happens to people, or even whole species, when they become unbalanced in one direction or the other. It is possible to look at a variety of qualities and define them as Dionysian or Apolline, which is a useful way to illustrate the necessary balance between the two. In music, for instance, melody and harmony could be considered Apolline while rhythm and dissonance could be thought of as Dionysian. A good tune, therefore, would have both sides of those qualities in some measure.

Here are some other examples to play with: wisdom and foolishness; light and dark; stress and relaxation; permanence and change; Platonic love and animal lust; study and playtime; *Thou Shalt Not* and *Do What Thou Wilt*.

It may be noticed by the more astute, though, that the spirit of Dionysos is rising again. Our western society has become increasingly Apolline in its outlook, with its increase in laws, anti-terrorist (or anti-communist, anti-German, anti-witch etc.) paranoia and the incredible rise of identikit consumer goods from identikit supermarkets for identikit customers. Dionysos is rising again to combat this imbalance.

The next section will look at those great men and women who have kept the Dionysian spirit alive and kicking throughout western history, the *Dionysian Heroes*.

Dionysian Heroes

Definitions

This section is about those great men and women through out the history of Western culture who can be considered heroes of the Dionysian Spirit. But, how does one define a Dionysian hero?

Ironically, such limiting definitions are Apolline in nature and lead us to the paradox of defining the indefinable. Having said that, without a definition we would have nowhere to start. Thus Dionysos and Apollo are again demonstrated as unable to exist alone, like Yin without Yang.

A Dionysian hero, then, would be someone who has exemplified the Dionysian spirit in their lives in some way. Usually through the media of the arts, music or philosophy these individuals have driven themselves and their culture forward towards greater freedom of expression, depth of feeling, liberation and passion of spirit. Sometimes they have been lauded during their lifetimes, more often their worth has remained unrecognised until after their deaths. Very often the Apolline powers of their societies have regarded them as cranks and lunatics or even dangerous criminals. Nevertheless, their activities have led us all to a greater sense of the Dionysian Spirit in our own lives, whether we have heard of them or not.

In writing this section I am indebted to the work of the philosopher/historian, Steve Ash, whose ideas and information I have cribbed from almost without mercy. Steve is a far better historian than I could ever hope to be, and I can only bow to his expertise.

Sadly, this cannot be a definitive list. To make such a list would be beyond the scope of this small volume and, frankly, boring for both the author and reader alike. If I have missed out your favourite or someone you feel should be here, I can only apologise. I make no apology, though, for the people I *have* included. In the final result the list is dependent on my own experiences and so must necessarily be a list of those who have impressed me in some way. Hopefully, they will impress you too.

Early Days

Unfortunately, the history of Western culture is cursed with a large gap. The period from the end of the Roman Empire to the European Renaissance is known as the Dark Ages with good reason. Due to the collapse of the Roman Empire, Europe regressed into feudal chaos and the only pan-European guardian of the arts was the increasingly powerful and Apolline Catholic Church. Life in the mediaeval period was, for the most part, miserable and strictly controlled, particularly for the vast majority poor[1]. Even in the upper echelons of society individualism and free-thinking were considered heretical and viciously suppressed. The Bible and church were considered the absolute and literal explanations of everything, even though most ordinary Christian people were not expected to read the bible or understand the catechism. Ancient works from the Classical period were kept hidden in monasteries by order of the Vatican.

It was not all bad, though. Christianity did not reach the Netherlands and Scandinavia until a fairly late date and took time in getting a foothold. Pagan attitudes and moralities therefore managed to remain in these areas for a little longer than most. The invading Vikings who caused so much trouble for British monasteries in the 10th century were Pagans and, whatever we think of their violent actions now, they brought with them a rich culture of celebration and personal liberty.

What little of the Dionysian Spirit that survived the slow holocaust of increasing church strength was kept alive by travelling minstrels and actors, and by the prevalence of fairs and chances to celebrate saints' days. Relatively late mediaeval bawdy stories such as those of Boccaccio's *Decameron* and Chaucer's *Canterbury Tales* give an indication of how individuals, whilst still in thrall to the church, could have a good time.

It is also arguable that some of the poor unfortunates who suffered during the witchcraft mania - which crossed the borders from the mediaeval to the early-modern period – were indulging in Dionysiac practises. The vast majority of witchcraft-related deaths in this period were likely to have been politically motivated: Catholics used accusations of witchcraft and devil-worship to persecute Protestants, Protestants used them to persecute Catholics. Witchcraft's name was used by landlords to get rid of unwelcome tenants, by bankrupt tenants to get rid of grasping landlords and by petty children to punish cantankerous old women.

Even so, it is possible that there were small and isolated enclaves of people who would cling to the leftovers of ancient celebratory practices involving sexual license and the use of mind-altering substances such as the famous "flying-ointment". It is quite likely that many of these would have turned to "the Devil" as an alternative to what the church taught.

As a philosophy put simply, one could say that living according to the rules of the church - worshipping God and Jesus - makes one poor, hungry and miserable. In fact, being poor, hungry and miserable are actually considered to be virtues. Why not, then, worship the Devil - the enemy of the church - in the hope that he will provide a better life, or a least a moment's ecstatic relief from drudgery and sickness, and from the starvation caused by taxation to fund wars in places you have never heard of? Such an idea looks especially likely during the 14th century, which was marked by climatic change, famine, the Black Death and the Hundred Years War.

The Renaissance and Onwards

One of the first great Dionysian heroes to come out of the Renaissance was the French writer, Francois Rabelais, or rather his wonderful, huge creation, Pantagruel. The five books concerning Pantagruel - strictly four concerning Pantagruel and one concerning his father, Gargantua - tell the story of the eponymous hero, a lustful superhuman giant. Pantagruel embodies the greatest of the Dionysian traits in his lust for life, experience, knowledge and, of course, alcohol. The satire within the novels has not, understandably, translated well from mid-16th Century France but the very straightforward, extremely earthy humour certainly has.

In *Gargantua*, Rabelais also used one of his lively characters, Friar John of the Hashes, to create what he considered the ideal society: the Abbey of Thélème. It was to be a religious order without outer walls or other restrictions, such as laws. Open to both men and women it was the ultimate in anarchistic fantasy where people would naturally rise to their highest ideals, free from the restrictions of law-and-order based social conditioning:

> "Enter not here, lawyers insatiable,
> Ushers, lawyers' clerks, devourers of the people,
> Holders of office, scribes, and Pharisees,
> Ancient judges who tie up good citizens
> Like stray dogs with a cord on their necks. . ."
> "Grace, honour, praise, and light
> Are here our sole delight;
> Of them we make our song.
> Our limbs are sound and strong.
> This blessing fills us quite,
> *Grace, honour, praise, and light*"[1]

The Abbey of Thélème had one rule and one rule only: "Do What You Will". Students of Aleister Crowley will probably find the concepts of *Thélème* and *Do What You Will* somewhat familiar. Crowley, at whom we shall look in more detail later, was a great fan of Rabelais and heavily influenced by his writings. The Sorbonne and the Roman Catholic Church, however, were not. Despite great popularity, academics and church leaders condemned Gargantua and Pantagruel for unorthodoxy, obscenity and the heresy of deriding religious practises.

The period following the Renaissance has since become known as the *Enlightenment* or the *Age of Reason*. It was during this period, ranging roughly from the end of the 17th Century through to the middle of the 19th that saw the rise of the industrial and political revolution, science and epistemological philosophies. One of the most important considerations of the Enlightenment is that it can be thought of as a change in human attitudes as much as in actual thought. The overriding belief was in *reason*, as opposed to passion or faith, as the greatest human quality.

The Enlightenment probably did produce its share of true Dionysians but history has done little to remember them when compared to such characters as Newton, Descartes and Thomas Jefferson.

The period following was an entirely different kettle of fish!

Romance

The end of the Enlightenment saw the upsurge of a new passion and romanticism in art and particularly in poetry. It allowed a new freedom of spirit into the daily lives of those fortunate enough to be able to appreciate it. In the middle of the 18th century the best compliment one could give was to call someone reasonable, a hundred years later the greatest thing was to say that someone had passion.

One of the precursors of this shift in emotional paradigm was the playwright and poet John Wilmot, 2nd Earl of Rochester. Played most admirably by Johnny Depp in the film, *The Libertine*[1],Wilmot was a creature very much ahead of his of time. He lived for only 33 years of the mid 17th century, dieing of syphilis, and he was a personal friend of the king, Charles II. His plays and poetry were known for their bawdy and satirical nature and the last play attributed to him, *Sodom or the Quintessence of Debauchery* was the cause of prosecutions for obscenity. Unfortunately, Wilmot's poetry was mostly unpublished until after his death and consequently had very little influence during his lifetime.

The ingress into the 19th century brought to light the work of two of literature's great Dionysians. The first of these, William Blake is well known, the second is a little more obscure: Mary Robinson.

Mary Robinson (née Darby) was a poet and actress born in 1758 to a sea captain and his wife and was the third of five children. Mary's love of the written word was encouraged by her mother who started a school after being abandoned by her husband. Her writing during her early life was barely noticed in comparison to her acting, particular her role as *Perdita* in *A Winter's Tale* which brought her a very modern kind of celebrity. She was spotted by, and became the mistress of, George IV, after a failed marriage at the age of 21.

Mary caught a debilitating disease when she was 26 which was to slowly destroy the rest of her life. Yet, at the same time, and although ignored by the literary establishment, she managed to produce several novels, a feminist treatise, two plays and an autobiography[2]. It seems that her Dionysian nature found its way beyond the limits of her body through literary expression, and a fifteen year affair with a soldier. She died, after many years of increasing ill-health in 1800 at the age of 42.

Mary Robinson has been sadly neglected since, both as a writer and as a Dionysian, but is currently experiencing a kind of after-life reprise. Here, to help add to that fame is her sonnet, *To Liberty*:

Oh! Liberty! transcendent and sublime!
  Born on the mountain's solitary crest;
Nature thy nurse, thy fire unconquered Time,
  Truth, the pure inmate of thy glowing breast!
Oft dost thou wander by the billowy deep,
  Scattering the sands that bind the level shore,
Or, towering, brave the desolating roar
  That bids the tyrant tempest lash the steep!
'Tis thine, when sanguinary daemons lour,
  Amidst the thickening hosts to force their way;
To quell the minions of oppressive power,
  And shame the vaunting nothings of a day!
Still shall the human mind thy name adore,
  Till chaos reigns—and worlds shall be no more!
(1796)

William Blake (1757-1827) was also relatively unknown during his lifetime but has since been given the recognition he most surely deserves. Blake was possibly Britain's greatest mystic and visionary. A deeply spiritual man and a devout but somewhat unusual Christian, he rejected the orthodoxy of the church as stultifying to the human spirit. He even created his own mythology to express his spiritual beliefs, particularly in *The Marriage of Heaven and Hell* which was heavily influenced by Milton's *Paradise Lost*, Dante's *Inferno* and the religious philosophy of Swedenborg. He not only wrote but also illustrated his own and other authors' books with engravings and watercolours.

Perhaps Blake's most famous writing is the lyric to Parry's hymn "Jerusalem", beloved of Women's Institute meetings everywhere. It is pleasing to believe that Blake, as a great believer in sexual and racial equality, would consider this an amusing compliment.

Because of his enormous and highly Dionysian output, and the limitations of space in this section, it is difficult to find a particular quotation to sum up the life and work of William Blake. Here, then, is a piece which is no more than a personal favourite from *Auguries of Innocence*:

> To see a world in a grain of sand,
> And a heaven in a wild flower,
> Hold infinity in the palm of your hand,
> And eternity in an hour.

The turn of the 19th century also saw the rise of the Romantic movement in poetry. The Romantic poets were precursors of the end of the Age of Reason in much the same way as Blake. They expressed and lived lives of passion and deep but unorthodox spirituality, and have become very much household names - Keats, Shelley, Coleridge, Wordsworth – but we are going to concentrate here on one character whose life epitomised the whole movement: Lord Byron.

Byron lived a life as full, riotous and short as any 1960s rock star. Born George Gordon in 1788, he inherited the title Lord Byron at the age of ten. His father, John "Mad Jack" Gordon Byron, was a sea captain who is thought to have married his mother, Catherine for money and then abandoned her. She took her son to Aberdeen where he spent his early years and education. His later education was at Harrow.

Byron's magnetic, flamboyant and highly dominating personality were probably the result of his privileged upbringing combined with the advantages of exceptional intelligence and the warring disadvantages of latent homosexuality and the physical disability of a club foot. He soon gained a reputation amongst his peers, being famously described by Lady Caroline Lamb as "Mad, bad and dangerous to know". He had numerous love affairs, both before and during marriage, and he also had an unfortunate tendency towards casual cruelty to ex-lovers who no longer interested him.

Byron chose to live in Europe to escape the censure of British society and moved around absorbing cultures and languages as he travelled. His final home became Greece where he had, despite having no military experience, become involved in the Greek war of independence from the Ottoman Empire. He died in 1824 at the age of 36 after catching a violent cold which was turned into a fever by the popular treatment of bleeding. He is considered a national hero in Greece to this day[3].

Despite having such a full life, Byron managed to write prolifically. He is even credited with the creation of a new literary archetype, the "Byronic Hero". Here is a verse from one of his last poems, *On This Day I Complete My Thirty-Sixth Year.*

If thou regret'st thy youth, why live?
The land of honourable death
Is here: - up to the field, and give
Away thy breath!

America

While the Romantics were suffering early deaths in Britain and Europe, the spirit of Dionysos had also taken root in the hearts of a few influential American writers and thinkers such as the transcendentalist, Ralph Waldo Emerson, the social reformer and feminist Margaret Fuller and arguably the most important American philosopher of all, Henry David Thoreau (1817-62).

In a Dionysian sense, Thoreau's work is incredibly important because it shows how individualism and libertarian ideals can be translated into daily life in a practical way. He campaigned for social reform, non-violent civil disobedience and the abolition of slavery throughout his adult life. It was his willingness to act rather than theorize which led him to take part in his greatest social experiment. For two years, two months and two days Thoreau dropped out of normal society and took up a contemplative life as a self-sufficient hermit in a small self-built cabin on the shores of Walden Pond, on the edge of woodland near Concord, Massachusetts.

He published his memoirs of this adventure in 1854 as *Walden, or Life in the Woods*. It was not popular during his lifetime but has since become considered an American classic. There is a particular quotation from *Walden* which expresses perfectly how the Dionysian spirit ran through Thoreau during his time on Walden Pond, and which anyone who has seen the film *Dead Poets' Society* will instantly recognize:

"I went to the woods because I wanted to live deliberately, I wanted to live deep and suck out all the marrow of life, To put to rout all that was not life and not when I had come to die discover that I had not lived."

Equally familiar to viewers of that same film should be the man who was possibly America's greatest ever poet, Walt Whitman.

Unusually for one with such a strong Dionysian influence, Whitman managed to live a long and productive life. He rarely even drank alcohol. He was born to Quaker parents in Long Island, New York in 1819 and died some time after suffering a stroke at the age of 72. Also unusually for such a Dionysian figure, Whitman lived long enough to gain popularity in his own lifetime and witness the changes he influenced. His funeral at Campden, New Jersey was preceded by a public viewing which had over a thousand visitors in three hours. It is said that the coffin could barely be seen for all the flowers and wreaths.[1]

Whitman was radical during his lifetime. He wrote mostly in free verse, which was highly unusual at the time, and his first collection, *Leaves of Grass*, was vilified for its sexual frankness (or "obscenity" as it was called in the popular press) but loved by his fellow poets and intellectuals such as Emerson, Thoreau and Alcott. He was also powerfully influenced by his experiences of nursing the wounded and dieing soldiers who fought in the American Civil War, a few of whom were his own brothers.

One may think that such a difficult life - as an impoverished printer in New York, a dreary civil servant in Washington, and irregular work at that — would leave Whitman bitter and unhappy. Indeed he did suffer from depression, but his poetry is almost entirely characterised by joy and love. This was not the ordinary quiet joy and love associated with, for instance a happy and satisfied marriage, but a huge, wild, all-encompassing yearning for nature and his fellow humans. His love of his fellow man has probably been misinterpreted as homosexuality. In the opinion of this author Whitman had little sexual interest at all, his heart being so big he could love man or woman with equal the power and vigour with which he loved the earth and sky. His own words say it better than anyone else possibly could, and I make no apologies for quoting him at length.

The atmosphere is not a perfume, it has no taste of the
distillation, it is odorless,
It is for my mouth forever, I am in love with it,
I will go to the bank by the wood and become
undisguised and naked,
I am mad for it to be in contact with me.
Clear and sweet is my soul, and clear and sweet is all that
is not my soul.
Every kind for itself and its own, for me mine male and
female,
For me those that have been boys and that love women,
For me the man that is proud and feels how it stings to
be slighted,
For me the sweet-heart and the old maid, for me
mothers and the mothers of mothers,
For me lips that have smiled, eyes that have shed tears,
For me children and the begetters of children.
My lovers suffocate me,
Crowding my lips, thick in the pores of my skin,
Jostling me through streets and public halls, coming
naked to me at night,
Crying by day, Ahoy! from the rocks of the river,
swinging and chirping over my head,
Calling my name from flower-beds, vines, tangled
underbrush,
Lighting on every moment of my life,

Bussing my body with soft balsamic busses,
Noiselessly passing handfuls out of their hearts and
giving them to be mine.
Do I contradict myself?
Very well then I contradict myself,
(I am large, I contain multitudes.)
I too am not a bit tamed, I too am untranslatable,
I sound my barbaric yawp over the roofs of the world.

All of the above are from the huge, rambling, exultant *Song of Myself*
which was published as part of his first and probably most important collection, *Leaves of Grass*. The following is my own favourite
poem:

When I hear'd the learned astronomer,
When the proofs, the figures, were ranged in columns
before me,
When I was shown the charts and diagrams, to add,
divide and measure them,
When I sitting heard the astronomer where he lectured
with much applause in the lecture-room,
How soon unaccountable I became tired and sick,
Till rising and gliding out I wander'd off by myself,
In the mystical moist night air, and from time to time,
Look'd up in perfect silence at the stars.

Germany

The spirit of Dionysos was at work strongly in the literature of Germany during the 19th Century. He rose to prominence through the work of the poet, Heinrich Heine during the early part of the century and via Oswald Spengler at the end. In between them came the man who could be considered Dionysos' most important and influential philosopher, Friedrich Nietzsche.

Heine (1797-1856) was an intellectual and student of Classical Mythology who, in the 1853 essay *The Gods in Exile* re-introduced Dionysos as a moral archetype similar to Blake's powerful heroes of the previous century. Spengler (1880-1936) was a historian and philosopher who, despite his extremely conservative and therefore Apolline views considered that a new form of Dionysian humanity was about to rise. In his book, *The Decline of the West*[1], he makes a statement which rings truer today than ever:

. . . western civilisation had degenerated into a shallow and artificial "mass culture" cut off from nature and based on false ideals, narrow rational utility and consumerism. A passive, rootless society shaped by illusions generated by marketers and the mass media. An alienating shell of a society with no sense of community, other than an internally competitive rule of the mob. In contemporary terms, an atomised chaos of competitive – but low achieving – conformist "clones", with no idiosyncrasy or deeper values than the latest consumer trend.

Friedrich Nietzsche is known nowadays as a German philosopher. In truth and in line with his ideals, he gave up his

Prussian and German citizenships and became stateless. Nietzsche was born in 1844, the son of a Lutheran pastor who died when his son was only 5 years old. Nietzsche was, consequently, brought up by his mother and grandmother. He lived a relatively successful life, working as a university professor and studying a variety of disciplines until failing health forced him to stop regular work around 1879. Throughout his life, he was plagued with debilitating and worsening eyesight problems, migraines and stomach attacks. Yet his is probably the most positive, life-affirming and optimistic of all the philosophies of his time. He was finally overtaken by a mental illness[2] in 1889 and was cared for by his mother and sister until his death in 1890.

Nietzsche used the Dionysian/Apolline dichotomy as the major theme in his early work, *The Birth of Tragedy*[3]. This book concerns the nature of Greek Tragedy as a formation based on the balance and interplay of Apolline order and structure (the hero) and Dionysian chaos (fate). The end result takes the audience into a Dionysian state of revelry and wonder. In later, more moralistic, books Nietzsche uses the imagery of the Dionysian as one who stands above and beyond herd-mentality and refuses to accept the Judaeo-Christian "slave-morality" of restraint, meekness and subservience.

Nietzsche's work is often poetic and difficult to interpret. There are even some who do not count him as a philosopher at all, but rather a faux-biblical poet. Nonetheless, his work has been arguably the most influential philosophy of the modern period. He has been blamed for the rise of everything from Nazi fascism to libertarian anarcho-pacifism. The following quote from the historian/

philosopher, Steve Ash explains Nietzsche's moral philosophy most succinctly:

Nietzsche's ideal human was the "Higher" or "Dionysian" man, who was an authentic, free spirit, in touch with their primal nature, who attempted to unify and "recreate themselves" by overcoming and sublimating their various drives into a unified whole of their own aesthetic choice (true being). The archetypal successful sublimator, and self-created being, was the (in)famous "Over-Man".

Turning the Century

Several characters carried the Dionysian spirit up to and across the turn of the 20th century. Not least of these were the French writers Rimbaud and Proust whose works expressed the intense and dazzling beauty of life to which mundanity, habit and familiarity have often left us blind.

By way of example, here is a translation of Rimbaud's short poem, *Departure*.

All is seen...
The vision gleams in the air.
All is had...
The distant sound of cities at night,
In sunlight, always.
All is known...
Chaos! Disorder!
These are the stuff of life.

Departure while love yet lingers,
And bright sounds.

Another remarkable and ground-breaking French individual of the period was the actress, Sarah Bernhardt (1844-1923). The Divine Sarah, as she became known, was not only an incredibly successful actress on both stage and screen, but also an immense self-publicist and notorious liar. Her success was put down to her talents as a courtesan as much as an actress, both of which were scandalous careers for a respectable woman. Nevertheless, and despite the loss of a leg, she became one of the most famous and accomplished women of her time – not only as an actress, but also as writer, artist and artists' muse. She cleared the path into French culture for the multitude of women who came after her.

In Britain the two most famous carriers of the Dionysian torch across the turn of the century were Oscar Wilde (1854-1900) and DH Lawrence (1885-1930). While being rather different people who wrote rather different literature they were both stigmatised for their works and attitudes.

Lawrence's fourth novel, *The Rainbow* was banned in Britain in 1915 on the grounds of obscenity and all extant copies were seized and burned. *Lady Chatterley's Lover* was not released until 1960, thirty years after the author's death, and was then the subject of a very famous obscenity trial[1]. Despite his wide variety of talents, Lawrence was seen as little more than a pornographer until relatively recently, but the uncompromising nature of his work and its acceptance has allowed and encouraged a much more open attitude to explicit writing in the western world since 1960.

The Irish writer, Oscar Wilde[2] is so famous as to need almost no introduction at all. Wilde mostly wrote and produced plays, poetry and short stories and became the most successful living playwright of his time. He was almost as famous for his biting wit as for his writing, which has become legendary, "*I think that God, in creating man, somewhat overestimated His ability.*" He was beaten only by Sarah Bernhardt. When asked by Wilde whether she would mind if he smoked she allegedly replied, "I don't care if you burn!"

In spite of its ending in keeping with the highly moral nature of literature at the time, Wilde's only novel, *The Picture of Dorian Gray* suffered an accusation of immorality. So did Wilde himself when, in 1895, he was sentenced to two years of hard labour for the crime of sodomy. He died at the age of 46 in self-imposed exile from society circles in Paris, which is where he wrote *The Ballad of Reading Gaol* about his imprisonment. Many of the lines have become famous in themselves:

> Yet each man kills the thing he loves
> By each let this be heard
> Some do it with a flattering look
> Some with a bitter word

While the influence of Oscar Wilde on modern culture is almost too large to be measured there were other Dionysians of the turn of the century who are rather less well known. Chief among these is the psychologist, Otto Gross (1877-1920).

Gross was an Austrian student of Sigmund Freud who later rejected Freud's theories in favour of an anti-psychiatric approach. He favoured methods involving depth psychology and sexual liberation and was accused of organizing orgies. He was also an anarchist, a feminist and a neo-Pagan who lived in a variety of communes and was deeply influenced by the works of Kropotkin, Nietzsche and Stirner. In his turn he influenced such luminaries as Franz Kafka, Willhelm Reich and the German Dada movement. His work is only now beginning to reach prominence[3].

The relative obscurity of Gross stands in contrast to his fellow Dionysian psychologist and ex-student of Freud, Carl Gustav Jung (1875-1961). Jung, after Freud, is probably the best known psychoanalyst of our time. Most important was his attempt to bring psychology into the realms of the unscientific, thus to blend and balance both the rational and irrational sides of the human psyche. He spent much of his life in the study of astrology, dreams and mythology as well as human psychology. It is Jung who has given the world such radical concepts as archetypes and the collective unconscious.

Jung also used the images of Dionysos and Apollo, taken directly from Nietzsche, in his understanding of the mind. Apollo would represent reason and logical thought, Dionysos would represent the deep and uncontrollable passions. The wholeness and psychological health of a person would depend on the integration of these two parts of the personality.

Divine Decadence, Darling!

During the First World War Dionysos' influence on Western Culture was, understandably, quiet. Battle requires discipline and obedience which are definitely not the most Dionysian of qualities. Between the two World Wars, however, his spirit lifted Europe and America to new levels of both creativity and debauchery.

One of the most important centres for the new Dionysiac was the German city of Berlin. After the War, and the consequent worldwide depression, Germany was in a great deal of trouble. The new Democratic Republic, based in Weimar was under siege from Communists, Nazis and Anarchists on all sides. There was politically motivated violence on the streets and an inflation rate so high money became worth less than the bag used to carry it. There was little respite from suffering, yet at the same time there was a vast and unprecedented explosion of artistic and literary creativity in Weimar Germany. A list of notable figures from the Weimar era reads like a *Who's Who* of early 20th Century cultural icons, including artists, architects, film-makers and film stars, musicians, philosophers and the radical scientists who founded quantum mechanics

Many of them found fame, pleasure and emotional release in *Das Kabarett*.

Cabaret began in Paris at the end of the 19th Century. Rather than employing the formality of normal theatre, Cabaret was performed in cafés where people could sit around tables and eat or drink whilst being entertained. By the 1920s Germany had made Cabaret its own, particularly as the Weimar government had removed any forms of censorship. For film fans, Marlene Dietrich's classic *The Blue Angel* (*Der Blaue Engel* - Josef von Sternberg, 1930) and, of course, Bob Fosse's superb 1972 *Cabaret* (a film of the 1966 play John Kander and Fred Ebb) give a surprisingly truthful and accurate portrayal of the Kabarett subculture:

> *". . . in 1932 Berlin, with satiric sketches, torch songs, transvestism and more. These shows had an intellectual punch which, with a few drinks, helped audiences push the harsh realities of life aside for a few hours."*[1]

It was the Dionysian Cabaret subculture which gave the world such luminaries as Bertolt Brecht and Kurt Weill, Marlene Dietrich, Greta Garbo and Paul Klee. The rise of the Nazi party in the 1930's took advantage of the popularity of Cabaret and turned it to its own propagandist ends. At this point a great deal of the most famous Weimar-era personalities, many of whom were Jewish, left for pastures new. America was a particularly favourite destination.

One extreme Dionysian character from Weimar Berlin deserves special mention. Anita Berber was a dancer, actress and prostitute who managed to scandalise even the jaded Berliners of the 1920's. She was known to appear in hotel lobbies wearing nothing but a sable wrap, a terrified pet monkey and a silver brooch full of cocaine.

Sadly, she was too extreme and, after suddenly giving up her twin addictions of cocaine and alcohol, she contracted tuberculosis. Anita died in 1928 at the age of 29. Her life has been celebrated and immortalised in Mel Gordon's play, *The Seven Addictions and Five Professions of Anita Berber.*

Berlin also nurtured another unusual Dionysian immigrant, the anti-art art movement, Dada. Dada began in Zurich - which was neutral - during the middle of the War and its anti-establishment nihilism had appealed very strongly to the disaffected and war-weary German intelligentsia by the official end of hostilities in 1918. The ideal of Dada was to destroy all culture, in order to begin again with a blank slate. Like many before and after them the Dadaists used shock tactics to produce a reaction within their audience and bring about a breakdown of old and ossified thought patterns. They created new types of music and theatre and pioneered methods still used nowadays by radical art and political groups.

Berlin Dada was more politically inclined than its versions in other European cities and consequently had less influence on art movements as a whole. The Berlin Dadaists were especially victimized by the Nazi government in its persecution of "decadent art". Many of the Berlin artists moved to New York and Paris. In Paris Dada evolved through its many members, particularly André Breton, into the 20th Century's most radical, influential and Dionysian art movement, Surrealism.

Surrealism had developed into a fully-fledged art movement in

Paris by 1924, and published its manifesto that year. The aim of Surrealism was:

". . . to express. . . the real functioning of thought. Dictation of thought in the absence of all control exercised by reason, outside of all aesthetic and moral preoccupation."[2]

To achieve this end the Surrealists used whatever means they deemed appropriate or necessary. Being highly influenced by the theories of Sigmund Freud they tended towards methods involving dream imagery, eroticism and non-conscious automatism. Automatic drawing and writing were particular favourites, as were any other methods which minimized the artist's conscious input and drew images from the subconscious mind. In fact, Surrealism was at first intended to be a literary movement , and it was primarily André Masson's automatic drawings which marked the acceptance of visual arts into the Surrealist methodology.

Many famous and influential artists and writers were involved with the Surrealist movement - including most of the older Dadaists. Well-known names not yet mentioned include Man Ray, René Magritte, Luis Buñuel and even Pablo Picasso (if briefly). However the prize for ultimate Surrealist and Dionysian must go to the Catalan Spaniard, Salvador Dalí.

Dalí was born in Figueres in 1904, the son of a strict disciplinarian lawyer father and a doting, stay-at-home mother. His mother encouraged his artistic leanings and in 1914 he attended a private art school, giving his first exhibition in 1918. His techinique and exceptional attention to detail were compared favourably by his peers to the Renaissance masters.

Around 1924, while studying in Madrid, he dedicated himself to the Metaphysical School of Art (as proposed by de Chirico) and experimented with Cubism and Dada. It was in Madrid that he befriended his later film collaberator, Buñuel and also showed early signs of his eccentric showmanship. In 1926 he delared that there was nobody at the faculty of the Academia de San Fernando competent to judge his work. Unsurprisingly, they threw him out. In that same year he travelled to Paris where he met his idol, Picasso. It wasn't until 1929 that Dalí joined the Surrealist movement officially, and it was then that he met his muse and future wife, Gala (Elena Ivanovna Diakonova). She was married to the poet Paul Éluard at the time, but the Surrealist movement also had radical and somewhat Rabelaisian views on love and marriage.

Dalí painted his most famous work, *The Persistence of Memory* , commonly known as *The Melting Clocks*, in 1931. This was just his most appealing painting out of many though, and he had already collaborated with Buñuel on the film *Un Chien Andalou* and begun to develop his famous "Paranoiac-critical method". Put simply, the method involves seeing things that are not there – as happens when one stares for long periods at any particular object or texture – and reproducing them. The result is a kind of double image which confuses the conscious mind by suggesting a connection between the two images. As a method for the Surrealist artist's hand to bypass the eye and go straight to the brain, it proved very popular.

As well as being an exceptional artist, Dalí was also a notorious and highly successful self-publicist. His famous moustache was only a small symptom of his powerful personality, as were the deliberate depictions of masturbation, faeces and sacreligious images, and the extreme violence in his films *Un Chien Andalou* and *L'Age D'Or* He once, in 1939 upon being ejected from the Surrealist movement by the ever-more autocratic Breton, declared "I am Surrealism!" As well as his paintings and sculptures he collaborated with Walt Disney and Alfred Hitchcock, and experimented with holograms and theatre design. He also wrote several self-adoring books including a deliberately shocking autobiography, *The Secret Life of Salvador Dalí* and a single novel, *Hidden Faces.*

Dalí died in Figueres in 1989 at the age of 84, in his own Theater-Museum, some seven years after the death of Gala. It is thought that his death was due to Parkinson's disease. Dalí, in an interview for the American news show *60 Minutes* once said, "Dalí is immortal, and will not die". Judging from his massive output, fame and incredible influence on the worlds of art, film and theatre, he may have been right.

During the 1920s America was suffering from the same economic depression as the one which was affecting Germany. It was, very much, a world-wide phenomenon. Unwisely, the American government became more totalitarian in its morality and banned alcohol. Unsurprisingly such a Draconian measure was a spectacular failure. Not only did it create a whole new class of criminal, but it led to the rise of the famous "speakeasy" drinking dens - which made the Mafia so much money - and America's gift to worldwide culture and sexuality, Burlesque.

This American version of Kabarrett, or "Burly-Q" as it became known, grew out of music-hall and vaudeville theatre, basing most of its entertainments on short comedic and musical acts with the addition of striptease. It is no shock to learn that the sexual element became the most popular part of the show. In its heyday 1920's burlesque drew a huge clientele (generally of men) from all levels of society. One club for example, Minsky's in New York, was so succesful that its owner opened up two more clubs[3].

By the 1930's Burlesque was on the wane due to a vast amount of over-regulation. In New York it became illegal for a woman to be naked onstage and move at the same time. The well-known *Tableaux Vivant*, consisting of groups of nude women holding "artistic" poses, managed to retain a certain amount of popularity but the art of the striptease entered a phase of slow decline.

Then came World War II.

The British Dionysians seem to have been fairly quiet during the inter-war period. The reason may have been that their voices were drowned out by the loud flamboyance of one man, Aleister Crowley.

There is a vast literature available nowadays on "The Great Beast", so a simple précis should suffice here. He was born Alexander Edward Crowley in 1875 into a strictly conservative and religious family of Plymouth Brethren. The Brethren, however, had no qualms about making money and so young Alexander was brought up quite rich with a large inheritance to look forward to.

It was in 1896, at Cambridge and after the death of his father, that he began his interest in occultism. A year later he had joined the Hermetic Order of the Golden Dawn, a group which he eventually both led and, arguably, destroyed. At Cambridge he also discovered sex, with both men and women, which was to remain an abiding interest for the rest of his life. The blending of Magick and sex became very much his speciality. Sadly his attitude to women was overpowering and abusive, an attitude which still comes through in his influence today. Fortunately, Crowley's more recent female followers have become influential themselves in reinterpreting his works in more pro-female ways..

It is believed by many that Crowley was normally a pleasant and healthy person, despite some difficulty in empathising with others' problems[4], until he underwent a dramatic change in Cairo in 1904, at the age of 29. He invoked the spirit of the Egyptian god, Horus who told him that a new aeon was beginning and that he was to be its prophet. He named his new religion *Thelema* (from Rabelais) and even brought out a "bible", the *Book of the Law*, which he claimed to have been dictated to him by an angel. The *Book of the Law* contains what are probably the most famous quotaions in modern occult history, the most famous being *Do what thou wilt shall be the whole of the Law* and *Every man and woman is a star*

Crowley's undoubted self confidence and huge intellect led him to dominate almost everyone around him and he appears to have become ever more selfish and abusive as he got older. Due to an extremely robust constitution he also managed to take quantities of drugs which would have killed a normal person, alternately becoming addicted to some substance and then breaking the addiction through willpower alone. Eventually his body and his associates could stand it no longer and he died a lonely heroin addict in a dreary Hastings boarding house at the age of 72.

Crowley could well be seen as a failure. He did not achieve his ultimate aims, regardless of his strengths and determination and his last words, perhaps an occultist's urban legend, are reported to be "I am perplexed". At the same time he could also be considered one of the most alive, colourful and Dionysian people of his generation. His influence on all the branches of modern occultism is so huge as to be unreckonable and in the 60 years since his death his legend has almost become an industry in itself.

Post-War 20th Century

As happened in WWI, the spirit of Dionysos took second place during the privations of WWII, but afterwards it seems to have acquired a vast amount of energy. This upsurge - barring a few late Surrealists in Europe such as George Bataille and until the vast popularity of television in the 60's and 70s - appears to have happened mostly in America. It found its first and most important post-war home in the writers and poets of the "Beat Generation" and particularly in their mentor and father figure, William Burroughs.

William Seward Burroughs (1914-97) was a writer, artist, social commentator and drug-experimenter. He can be considered the father of the modern Dionysian current and, in his own way as influential as William Blake. Whether they know it or not, just about everybody in radical culture since 1945 has been influenced by Burroughs' work in some way. As well as campaigning (unsuccessfully) for a sensible approach to narcotic use in America for many years, he also introduced the world to the literary and artistic techniques of *cut-up* and *non-linear narrative*. Cut-up is not his own invention. Legend has it that it was created by Burrpough's friend, Brion Gysin who gave it to him as a gift. His most famous novel *Naked Lunch*, albeit written mostly under the influence of heroin, was the pioneer work of non-linear narrative. You can quite literally start and finish anywhere in the text and it will make as much (or little!) sense as if you had read it conventionally. For those who have never read Burroughs' work, the famous Quentin Tarantino film, *Pulp Fiction* is an excellent example of non-linear narrative.

Burroughs greatest influence was most certainly on the Beat Generation writers Jack Kerouac and Alan Ginsberg. He introduced Kerouac to Dionysos as a cultural and social archetype, and appears – under a pseudonym such as *Old Bull Lee* - in several of his novels. He and his then wife Joan Vollmer, who he later accidentally shot, also lived with Kerouac and Edie Parker in New York in 1944, before travelling across most of the U.S.A., and living in Tangier, Paris and London. His personal tastes and friendships with Ginsberg and Jean

Genet were also used as powerful influences in the lobby to legalise homosexuality in the 1960's.

Buuroughs influence and popularity among the avant-garde continue right up to the present day, and will probably carry on doing so. His admirers include William Gibson, Angela Carter, Patti Smith and Robert Anton Wilson amongst a whole raft of others both famous and obscure. On a personal level, I believe his funniest legacy comes in the name of the rock band, Steely Dan, who called themselves after a dildo in *Naked Lunch*.

Burroughs' last public appearance was in 1997, a few weeks before his death at the age of 83 of a heart attack. He was filmed pushing a shopping trolley containing a large spotlight in the band, U2's video for their song *Last Night on Earth*. The video finishes with a close-up of Burroughs' eyes.

Two of Burroughs' protogées have also had a profound effect on the Dionysian current in modern America and Britain, these being the previously mentioned authors, Jack Keroac and Alan Ginsberg. In particular, Kerouac's writings have become increasingly popular since his death and many are now considered classics of American literature.

Jack (or Jean Louis Kirouac, known to his mother as Ti' Jean) was born to French Canadian immigrant parents in Lowell, Massachusetts in 1922. He was brought up as a Roman Catholic, speaking Quebec French and started to learn English at the age of 6. He always spoke French at home, and his most famous novel, *On The Road* was also originally begun in French.

He was known to romanticize his early life and ancestry, making a variety of claims concerning both his lineage and the origin of his surname. He claimed aristocratic Breton and native American descent, as well as Norman and Irish. He even stated once that Kerouac was Irish for *Language of the Water*[1].

During his early life there were two events which steered Kerouac towards a career in writing. The first, as a child, was the very early death of his brother, Gérard of rheumatic fever which affected him deeply. The second was an accident on the sports field. At Columbia University he was both a sports writer for the student newspaper and something of a sports star in his own right, as a 100 meter hurdler and a running-back in the University's American Football team. Unfortunately for Jack, but of benefit to the rest of the world, he fractured his tibia in his first year. That, combined with a personality clash with his coach pulled him away from the sports field and towards the typewriter.

Kerouac dropped out of university and began his adventurous life in New York with his girlfriend, Edie Parker. He became embroiled in a murder after helping a friend, Lucien Carr dispose of evidence after Carr killed an obsessive and aggressive stalker, David Kammerer. He was arrested as a material witness and promised to marry Edie if she would pay his bail. The marriage lasted only a year, but it was during this period that Jack met most of the people who would be influential over the rest of his life, including Burroughs, Ginsberg, Herbert Hunke and most importantly Neal Cassady.

Kerouac also joined the U.S. Navy but was honourably discharged on psychiatric grounds.

Neal Cassady is the hero of the marvellous, intense, rambling and chaotic *On the Road*. This autobiographic novel covers a series of trips across America and is swimming in the subculture of jazz, benzedrine, alcohol and spiritual experiment, as are all Kerouac's most successful novels. Cassady features as the powerful but ultimately flawed Dionysiac hero, Dean Moriarty – a *holy goof*, a *saint, angel and devil*, the *Soul of Beat*[2]. Kerouac also created an entirely new, spontaneous and confessional writing style in *On the Road* by taping sheets of paper into a huge roll which he could feed directly into the typewriter and not have to break his flow by changing paper.

It is this spontaneity and energy which runs through Kerouac's work which makes him such a powerful Dionysian influence. His joy and lust for life and spiritual experience fill his novels with a rich wealth of imagery far outside the normal, mundane activities of a ordinary reader's life yet still accessible to everyone.

> . . . I see a vision of a great rucksack revolution
> thousands or even millions of young Americans
> wandering around with rucksacks, going up to mountains
> to pray, making children laugh and old men glad, making
> young girls happy and old girls happier, all of 'em Zen
> Lunatics who go about writing poems that happen to
> appear in their heads for no reason and also by being
> kind and also by strange unexpected acts keep giving

visions of eternal freedom to everybody and to all living creatures[3].

Unfortunately such energy was impossible for Kerouac to sustain over a long period, especially with a very strong alcohol habit, and he hated his celebrity status. In 1958 he hid himself away to look after his ailing mother and concentrate on writing novels and poetry. He died, outlived by his mother and his third wife, Stella, in 1969 at the age of 47. The cause was internal bleeding caused by a lifetime of heavy drinking.

One of the few long-term survivors of the Beat Generation was Kerouac's friend and occasional fellow traveller, Alan Ginsberg.

Born in 1926 in New Jersey and raised by fairly radical Jewish parents, Ginsberg grew up with a strong political and social ethic, and with a deep sympathy for mental illness from his mother who suffered from paranoia and epilepsy. He was also powerfully influenced by the works of Walt Whitman and his teacher's passion for poetry.

At Columbia University he met Lucien Carr who introduced him to, among others, Kerouac and Burroughs. Carr also introduced him to Neal Cassady which was the beginning of a long infatuation on Ginsberg's part. It was an unfortunate infatuation in many ways because Cassady was completely heterosexual, and had no interest in experimentation with men. Ginsberg did occasionally attempt forays into heterosexuality, but they were really against his nature and short-lived. In San Francisco in 1954 he met his fellow poet and life-long lover and partner, Peter Orlovsky.

In 1955 one of the defining events of the beat generation writers took place in San Francisco. Known as the *Six Gallery Reading*, it brought together radical poets from both the East and West coasts of America and was also the début of Ginsberg's most famous poem, *Howl*. The event was of such importance and excitement that Kerouac chronicled it in *The Dharma Bums*, describing collecting change for wine and Ginsberg reading drunk and ecstatic with his arms flung wide. The poem was also briefly banned on obscenity grounds after its official publication in 1956, but the ban was rescinded when the judged considered it to have redeeming social importance.

Ginsberg published a lot of poetry and was involved in many spiritual and social concerns in his long and full life, writing right up to his death in 1997 at the age of 70. He was involved in the anti-Vietnam war movement, gay rights, free speech and drug decriminalisation. In the end, though, his greatest legacy to the Dionysian Spirit can only be his incredible poem, *Howl*. The poem is far too long to reproduce in full, so here are a few selected lines. The reader is encouraged to seek it out in its full, three-part version.

I saw the best minds of my generation destroyed by
madness, starving, hysterical, naked,
Dragging themselves through the negro streets at dawn
looking for an angry fix,
Angelheaded hipsters burning for the ancient heavenly

connection to the starry dynamo in the machinery of
night
Who bared their brains to Heaven under the El and saw
Mohammedan angels staggering on tenement roofs
illuminated
Who talked continously seventy hours from park to pad
to bar to Bellevue to museum to the Brooklyn Bridge,
Who studied Plotinus Poe St. John of the Cross
telepathy and bop kabbalah because the cosmos
instinctively vibrated at their feet in Kansas,
Who thought they were only mad when Baltimore
gleamed in supernatural ecstasy.

Our temporal journey has now brought us now to the 1960s, a
period in which the Dionysian current became a raging torrent across
the Western world. The last 50 years or so have seen such a huge
uprising of the Dionysian spirit in popular culture that they will need
to be given a chapter of their own.

Before closing, though, perhaps it would be appropriate to name
one final hero of the 1960s who typified the blazing glory, extreme
excesses and utter self-destruction of the untamed Dionysian spirit.

My own choice would be the poet, singer, shaman and holy
lunatic, Jim Morrison. I recommend looking him up!

Dionysos Around the World

The generally accepted belief is that Dionysos is an Ancient Greek, or at least Near-Eastern god. In the normally accepted sense this belief is true enough, although we have looked at the fine details in section 1. Yet at the same time Dionysos has appeared in other guises in other cultures across the world. His influence has spread across the whole world, partly as the influence and worship of the god himself has spread and partly because his principles and gifts of *entheos* and *ekstasis* are natural factors in the human condition.

India

According to the myths, Dionysos travelled as far as India in his wanderings and missionary zeal, much like Alexander the Great did rather later. He is also said to have taken his worship and the culture of the vine with him. Having started in Turkey or Syria he would have passed through what are now known as Iraq, Iran and Pakistan, and possibly even Afghanistan leaving a Dionysian influence in his wake.

Due to the exceptionally powerful influence of Islam in these areas remnants of Bacchic culture are likely to be hard to find and so we will come back to them later. However once we reach the Indus Valley, now mostly in modern Pakistan and one of mankind's earliest city-based settlements, we begin to meet the Hindu gods. One of these in particular has some remarkable similarities to Dionysos, both in terms of legend and worship. His name is Shiva.

Modern Hinduism has many, many gods, but in something of a simplified form it can be considered to have three major gods, along with their consorts. These are Brahma, the creator; Vishnu, the preserver; and Shiva, the "destroyer". It is difficult for the modern Western Christianised mind to fully comprehend, because we often consider destruction to be "evil", but in the rigidly defined and thoroughly Apolline structure of traditional Hindu society and religion Shiva is considered by many to be the most important god of all. Destruction is another way of saying *transformation*, and this is where Shiva's vast importance and his similarities to Dionysos begin.

Many historians consider Shiva to have already existed as a god in Northern India prior to the influx of the Vedic peoples (before 2,000 BCE)[1] and that he blended with the Vedic storm god, Rudra. He may also be considered historically, like many gods, as a composite of multiple local gods. This is important because it directly relates Shiva to very ancient pre-Indo-Aryan culture and thus, according to many sources, pre-patriarchy in India.

But, he is so much more than dry historical analysis can give us and his attributes and associations bear this out.

As well as being known as Rudra ("roarer"), Shiva is also known as Bharaiva ("terrible"), Sundareshvara ("beautiful lord") and Nataraja ("lord of the dance"). His sacred animal is Nandi, the white bull and His most sacred symbol is the Lingam, or phallus. He wears a tiger skin and carries a snake.

The use of marijuana (or ganja, from "Ganges") is associated with his worship along with a number of other intoxicants, particularly the legendary Soma[2]. Nobody is entirely certain exactly what Soma is except that it is a drink with divine properties, or to put it more bluntly, some kind of drug - such as amanita mushrooms or ephedra juice. On top of all this, Shiva is also the patron god of Tantra, the most hidden and least well-understood of Hindu philosophy and practise, the religious art of sexual ecstasy.

The greatest similarities to Dionysos can be found in Shiva's aspect as Nataraja – the Lord of the Dance.

If you look carefully at an image of Shiva Nataraja (the famous dancing statue) you will see that he's not entirely male. He wears both male and female jewellery to indicate this dual nature and his connection to both the feminine and masculine aspects of divinity. It is entirely possible that this image of Shiva was, in origin, female or even hermaphroditic. He dances on the back of a dwarf or goblin-like creature which represents ignorance, and he is surrounded by a circle of flames and carries a drum, illustrating the moment-by-moment destruction and recreation of the universe.

His dance is like the dance of the Bacchante whose ecstatic movements take her to universal unity and gnosis. We have an image in the West of Indian religious worship being one of pure meditation and stillness, yet to the Shaivite dance is equally or more important. Dance is used to produce trance and ecstatic states, just like everywhere else in the world, and so to dance with Shiva is to become one with Shiva and achieve yoga.

Also on the sub-continent, but particularly the Tamil areas of southern India there is another god, lesser known in the west, who also carries something of the Dionysian spirit. He is known as Skanda, Murugan, Kartikeya or Subrahmanya, popularly considered the son of Shiva.

Skanda also hails from the Indus valley and his worship is thought to extend at least as far back as the 10th century BCE. As a deity he does not bear any great resemblance to Dionysos, except in his rites and rituals. He is a deity of the common people who can petition and worship him directly, and in Tamil Nadu his rites involve animal sacrifice and trance dancing. The most intense and ecstatic Tamil worshippers in Sri Lanka pierce their cheeks with skewers known as *vels*, or drag carts of holy statues through the streets by hooks pierced through the flesh of their backs.

China

The religious and spiritual life of China can be split into three basic but interweaving strands. These are Buddhism, Confucianism and Taoism. Buddhism was imported from India and blends quite well with both Taoism and Confucianism to the point where many of their philosophies are indistinguishable. Taoism and Confucianism, on the other hand, are very much in opposition.

Confucianism is a complicated system of rules and regulations by which life is to be governed, and Confucius himself was a high-ranking civil servant who lived around 500BCE during China's Han Dynasty. This was a period, philosophically speaking, of great expansion and experiment in China. It was known as the Hundred Schools period and brought forth many great and interesting philosophies, and advances in medicine, mathematics and other disciplines, as well as producing China's two most famous native thinkers.

Unfortunately nobody has ever found any writings which can be definitely ascribed to Confucius, but there are many writings and collections which have been attributed to him. Most of them are extremely conservative, rigorous and ritualistic in their attitudes

Confucius stressed experience, virtue and reasoned argument above all other considerations and it was really his later followers who turned his thoughts into the elaborate and complicated rules and regulations which became Confucianism. In modern China the influence of Confucianism, in the strict adherence to authority and minute regulation of daily life, has allowed Communism such a powerful sway over the population. Confucianism can be seen as one of the most successful Appoline philosophies ever created.

The Dionysian opposite to such a harsh and unyielding method is, of course, Taoism.

The roots of Taoism are ancient and deep, and can be traced right back to the earliest tribal and shamanic cultures in China. What we know of Taoism nowadays, though, is normally taken from the wonderfully poetic and mystical Tao Te Ching and the works of previous and subsequent writers.

The Tao Te Ching is said to have been written by the venerable sage, Lao Tzu (lit: *Old Master*), a contemporary of Confucius and a librarian in the Chou court in Lo-yang. Legend says that when Lao Tzu retired from court life he journeyed through a pass to the West of Lo-yang and stayed for some time with the Keeper of the Pass discussing the Tao and Taoist philosophies. The Keeper of the Pass refused to allow him to leave without writing his wisdom down for future generations. This writing became the Tao Te Ching, often translated into English as *The Classic of the Way*, a small volume of 81 short "chapters". Each chapter contains a spiritual or ethical aphorism or consideration in a very concise form. Some of the chapters are no more than forty words long.

The problem with the codification and writing down of any philosophy or belief is that it tends to become rigid and ossified. This has happened most dramatically with the Koran in the Western and Near-Eastern worlds, which some believe should not even be read in translation. The Tao Te Ching, though, has the distinct advantage of being exceptionally and beautifully vague, and therefore open to the widest of interpretation. Here is the first line, by way of example:

"Tao called Tao is not Tao"[1]

Taoism can be likened to Dionysian activity by its individualism, its lack of any organised structure and its tendencies towards feminism and libertarianism. The dominant philosophy in China has always been Confucianism, but it has ever been opposed by Taoism and many of China's greatest revolutionaries were Taoists. Such a one would be Chen Wang Ting, a Ming general on the losing side in the war with the Qing dynasty in 1644. He retired into hiding in his family village and there, using the Taoist principles of softness, *wu wei* ("do no thing") and flowing like water, developed the first Taoist martial art, Tai Chi Chuan.

The way of Tao is considered by many to be tuning into and following the way of nature. Such philosophy has led Taoists to consider male and female as equals in the world - which has always been a very unusual attitude in China - and in sexual matters women are generally considered the superior gender. Understandably then, Taoism has developed its own form of Tantra in which both parties can achieve ecstatic states and prolong their healthy lives. As with most Tantric methods there are no specific rules about being married or heterosexual, especially for women, and it is down to the individual to act as their consciences dictate. Also understandably, the moralist ruling Confucian elite have always found this abhorrent and have attempted to suppress Taoism periodically over the centuries, often with a great deal of violence.

Taoists can laugh at the Confucians though. In Chinese thought Taoists have pioneered the use of humour to break down linear-logical thought and to free the spirit. There is a famous Chinese painting much talked about by Western Orientalists, called *The Vinegar Tasters*. The picture features three men who have just tasted from a vat. One has a miserable expression, one has a sour, hard face and one is almost crying with laughter (although that is hard to tell on the actual painting). They represent China's three main religions and the vinegar represents life. Thus the Buddha is miserable because to him life is suffering which must be escaped, while Confucius is sour and hard because life is harsh and must be controlled. Lao Tzu, on the other hand, is about to collapse in a fit of giggles. Life, to him, is rich and wonderful and full of surprises, event if it does taste dreadful.

Modern Taoists are also helping to keep up this wonderful tradition of humour by writing such marvellous books as *The Tao of Pooh* (by Benjamin Hoff), which argues that A.A. Milne's Pooh Bear may well be the world's greatest Taoist. He probably is!

Taoism's most Dionysian school of thought has to have been the Drunken Dragons, or Seven Sages of the Bamboo Grove[2], which history places at around 250CE. They were a group of sages and poets who believed that the Tao could be achieved by drunkenness and general debauchery. They were very much a group of intellectuals who would spend all day talking and discussing the Tao and then drink until they achieved it. The most famous was Liu Ling, a very well-off upper-class gentleman who had a servant who would follow him around carrying a jug of wine and a spade. The former he kept should his master become thirsty and the latter in case his master dropped down dead during a binge.

Finally, it would be remiss not to mention Taoism's second best-known, and most prolific ancient writer Chuang Tzu. He lived about 200 years after Lao Tzu and was renowned for his ironic sense of humour and his belief in *wu-wei*, which means an attitude of flowing with nature rather than striving against it. Here is an excellent quotation from Chang Tzu to complete this section:

The purpose of words is to convey ideas. When the ideas are grasped, the words are forgotten. Where can I find a man who has forgotten the words? He is the one I would like to talk to

Africa

Europeans and Americans are taught from a very early age to consider the continent of Africa, south of the Sahara desert, as a primitive and uncivilised place. The Eurocentric version of history takes no account of the huge size of black Africa, nor its immense and multi-layered history. The fact that, until relatively recently in human history, sub-Saharan Africa was cut off from most of the rest of the world does not really help either. But European historians and archaeologists are beginning to re-appraise their ideas and to work with their African counterparts to rewrite a few of the history books.

We know, for instance, that there was an iron-age culture at some point in Nigeria, which apparently had moved directly from the stone-age without the usual intervening bronze[1]. The followers of Santeria, of whom we will hear a little later, talk of the sacred Yoruba city of *Ile Ife* in south-western Nigeria which has existed as an urban area since about 500CE, and still does . We also know that Ghana was a very rich country with trading links to the Arab world from around 300CE[2].

Zimbabwe (literally meaning "stone dwelling") was a huge city, empire and trading state between 1000-1600CE. When the ruined area was colonised by the white European Rhodesians in the late 1800s they refused to believe that indigenous people could have built the city[3] and claimed that it must have been of Arab or Hebrew origin. It was later proven to be of native construction and when the country returned to non-colonial rulership in 1980 the name was changed back to Zimbabwe.

Finally, Ethiopia has been considered one of mankind's oldest consistently settled areas. There were city states in Nigeria at the same time as those of ancient Egypt, it appears in the Iliad and Odyssey, and Ethiopia is referred to in the Bible as the "Land of Cush" along with Egypt. The oldest definite civilisation found in the area by archaeologists is the native civilisation known as the D'mt, which was established around 700BCE[4].

So where does Dionysos come in all this? Officially, of course, he does not, but his spirit is and always has been very much alive on the "Dark Continent".

The native religions of sub-Saharan Africa are primarily polytheistic and animistic in nature. The belief in spirits is almost universal and most practices involve some sort of communion between humans and these spirits. Usually this is performed in the same way as shamanism is elsewhere, in that the practitioner or a group of worshippers enter an ecstatic state which allows them to communicate with the spirit world or, more often, allows the spirit world to communicate through them.

Many tribes and traditional nations have even managed the rather nifty trick of combining the Dionysian method with an Apolline result. Prayers and sacred dances are performed by the whole group (say, a village or a club of young men) and the resulting shared ecstatic states and spiritual experiences are used to improve social cohesion and loyalty to the group rather than the individual.

When the trans-Atlantic African slave trade was at its height in the mid 18th century many hundreds of thousands of West Africans were taken to the New World to work the new plantations of cotton and sugar. They came mostly from Ghana, Nigeria, Senegal and other countries along the Atlantic coast. As was the practise of the time they were forcibly converted to Christianity but, unsurprisingly, like any repressed peoples they kept up their own indigenous ways as much as possible, partly as rebellion and partly as a way of keeping their identity as human beings. These beliefs and rituals were performed and passed on in secret. Eventually, as the children and grandchildren of the first slaves were brought up with a kind of dual spirituality, the African ways became fused with Christian ones to the extent that African gods and spirits became identical to the saints and heroes of the imposed Christianity.

On the island of Haiti this became known as *Voodoo*, from *Vodun* which was a name given to the native practices of coastal Ghana and Nigeria. In Cuba the religion became *Santeria*, a direct descendant of the Nigerian Yoruba traditions. Both of these religions spread into America proper and are now disseminating around the globe. This author has personally met a British Yoruba practitioner in, of all places, the coastal resort of Blackpool.

Voodoo and Santeria are extremely similar in outlook and method, the main differences being in the terminology, such as the names of deities, which is used. There are almost identical religions in Brazil, which is known as *Candomblé Jejé,* and the Dominican Republic where they have their own form (and spelling) of *Vudu.*

The basic principles of Voodoo method are ekstasis and entheos - ecstasy and enthusiasm in their truest senses. The rituals are open to both genders and led by a priest known as a *Hougan,* or a priestess called a *Mambo.* The basic tenet is that there is a supreme god, who takes no part in human affairs, and many "saints" or *Loa* with whom the practitioner interacts and who intercede with the supreme being where necessary. The Loa are invoked by various kinds of drumming, dancing, singing, feasting and so on, and the dancers enter an ecstatic state in which a Loa will take possession of them and speak through them. This is known as "being ridden by the Loa" and is literally identical with our concept of enthusism. It is often quite a violent and disconcerting experience.

A voodoo ritual is also reminiscent of the Bacchanalia in that it is totally democratic. The Loa will not necessarily choose to ride a priest or priestess, but will happily possess any dancer or member of the audience. It is not considered unusual for a twenty-stone bearded trucker to channel the coquettish love-Loa, Erzulie, or a small girl to become possessed by the mighty and thoroughly masculine Ogoun.

When a Loa rides a worshipper they act in a manner specific to that Loa, which is the priest's job to recognise, and then the other worshippers will give them whatever they may need. Baron Samedi, for instance, has a nasal voice and laughs loudly while making broad and often crude jokes. He requires a pair of sunglasses from which he will push out the right lens, rum and lots of cigarettes or cigars. The protective snake-Loa, Dumballah, on the other hand, will make soft hissing sounds radiating a sense of gentle optimism, and requires an egg which he will break with his teeth.

Once the Loa have been called and fed they will perform services for the worshippers such as answering questions, giving advice or curing ills.

Of course not all of the African slaves kept to their original heritage and many, or at least many of their descendants became true and honest converts to Christianity. Interestingly though, the most popular black American churches have done so in a very African and Dionysian style. These are the rather wonderful Gospel churches which, totally unlike the cold and dreary formalised Protestant and Catholic styles, have highly emotional rituals involving the whole congregation. The Christianized versions of ecstasy and enthusiasm, such as free-form personal expressions of faith like dancing and speaking in tongues, are positively encouraged in Gospel worship. In many ways the modern Gospel congregation is very much an image of what the first Christian churches must have been like.

Finally, Afro-American culture has also given us our modern form of the Mardi Gras. While the Catholic church in Europe first instigated the early spring carnivals, although almost certainly basing them on earlier Pagan models like the Saturnalia, it was Afro-America's adoption of "Fat Tuesday" and the subsequent world-wide influence of a bloody good party which has led to the colourful, loud and thoroughly Dionysian Mardi Gras parades we enjoy today.

Judaism

The natural exuberance and joyous impiety of the Dionysian spirit can pop up in some of the most unexpected places. Orthodox Judaism is one of those unexpected places.

As most Biblical scholars will know, Judaism is a religion based almost entirely on strict rules, regulations and tradition. Not only are there the famous Ten Commandments, there are an awful lot of smaller, less famous Biblical commandments (*mitzvot*, of which there are 613 in total) which must be explicitly obeyed. Many of these are extremely specific, many others are quite vague and open to interpretation. They can be broken down into laws concerning the Sabbath, family purity, sexual conduct, dietary rules and so on, all of which are defined and interpreted in a sort-of secondary Bible known as the *Talmud*.

Yet somewhere in all the rigid, Apolline restriction there is room made for some Dionysiac freedom and revelry. As well as the use of a little wine at almost all Jewish celebrations, there is also the feast of *Purim*, a festival based around the Book of Esther.

The Book of Esther, also known as the *Megillah*, has the surprising honour of being the only book in the Bible (Jewish *Tanakh* or Christian Old Testament) which makes absolutely no mention of God. Instead it tells the story of how the Persian king Ahasuerus -

having removed his wife for having a mind and will of her own - takes the pretty young orphan Esther to become his new wife. Esther has been fostered by her uncle Mordechai and both of them are, unbeknown to the king, Jewish. Mordechai reveals a plot to kill the king, which puts him in favour at court. The king, however, is not informed of this.

King Ahasuerus then brings in the character of Haman to be his prime minister. Since Mordechai offends Haman by refusing to bow to him and is subsequently discovered to be Jewish, Haman - with Ahasuerus' permission - orders that all the Jews in the state are to be killed. He draws lots (which is where the word, *Purim* comes from) to decide the date for the genocide – the 13th day of the month of Adar.

Mordechai asks Esther to intercede with the king on the Jews' behalf, although this would mean risking her own life by appearing before the king uninvited and revealing that she herself is Jewish. Mordechai also orders all the Jews to fast and pray for Esther and their own salvation.

Eventually, after much persuasion and accidentally discovering that it was Mordechai who saved his life, the king relents. He orders great honours for Mordechai at a feast with Haman present. He also discovers that his wife is Jewish, as is her uncle, and that it is his wife's people who are to be exterminated. In a rage he leaves the room, only to return to find Haman begging Esther to persuade the king to spare his life. Mistakenly thinking that Haman is assaulting the queen, Ahasuerus orders Haman hanged on the gallows he'd built for Mordechai.

Unfortunately the order to kill all the Jews is unable to be annulled, but instead the Jews are allowed to defend themselves and consequently Haman's ten sons are killed in the fighting, along with 500 other attackers. Mordechai is rewarded with a prominent position at court and institutes an annual celebration of the events of 13th Adar.

According to many writers, the Book of Esther is clearly a political revision of a much earlier myth concerning the goddess, *Ishtar*. In fact, Esther is simply the Hebrew pronunciation of Ishtar, Haman may relate to a Persian demon and Mordechai is almost certainly the Babylonian god, *Marduk*. It's highly likely, then, that the festival of Purim is directly descended from an extremely popular Persian/Babylonian festival which the Levitical priesthood simply could not get rid of without having a revolution on their hands. Sensibly it was allowed to continue and slowly evolve into something rather more Jewish than Babylonian.

All of this would be mere academic conjecture were it not for the activities indulged in during Purim. The author personally recommends spending time people-watching in a well-populated Jewish area on the day of Purim, because it is immense fun. It is, first and foremost, a Spring celebration. There are children's parties and kids dressed up as characters from the Megillah are a common sight, especially little boys with huge, painted-on moustaches and tinfoil swords. Special cakes are baked, known as *Hamantaschen*, (literally, "Haman's ears") which may have some relation to a folk memory of "baking cakes for the Queen of Heaven"[1].

The most important aspect of Purim, though, is drinking. Although in many communities it is considered to apply only to men, it is actually a law (*mitzvah*) to get extremely drunk at Purim. Nearly every Orthodox Jewish household in the world has a story of Uncle Solly (or someone similar) dancing on the table at Purim.

The Book of Esther is read out in Synagogue twice on the day of Purim, once in the morning and once in the evening, and it is the job of the congregation to cheer rowdily for Mordechai and loudly boo at Haman all the way through. The ideal is that, by the time the evening reading comes one should be so drunk as to be incapable of telling the difference and so cheer and boo in the all wrong places. This can get rather raucous and confusing, particularly when one considers that the Megillah is read in Hebrew and most European Jews do not use Hebrew as a day-to-day language. They have to concentrate quite hard to fully comprehend the story under normal circumstances. When drunk it is all but impossible.

The Arabic-Islamic World

Nowadays North Africa, the Middle-East and much of the area between Russia and India are almost entirely controlled by the various forms of Islam, ranging from moderate rule in holiday destinations like Tunisia and Turkey to extremist hard-line regimes such as the absolute monarchy of Saudi Arabia or the recently ousted Taliban of Afghanistan.

Islam, like Judaism, is very much a religion of rules and strictures, one of the most famous being the condemnation of alcohol[1]. If you believed that you would be hard-pressed to find a Dionysian streak in the Arabic/Islamic world, you would be completely correct. Nonetheless, it is there. It is hidden, quiet and suddenly popping up in unexpected ways, but it is there.

Islam is similar to Christianity in that it has either invaded or been imported into the vast majority of countries where it holds sway. Also like Christianity it has had to adapt to those countries in order to be accepted, often by adopting some of the pre-existent customs. An example would be the Persian New Year, *Nowruz*, which has been celebrated in Syria (Iran) on the day of the Spring Equinox for well over 3,000 years. Islam has adopted Nowruz in much the same way as the early church in Europe adopted Samhain and converted it into Hallowe'en. In Iran Nowruz has kept its traditional nature even to the extent of including a person playing a sacrificial figure representing an ancient Sumerian god.

The Kurds in Turkey also celebrate Nowruz with fairground outings and huge bonfires which are danced around and leapt over.

One of the most wonderfully Dionysian books ever to be written came, rather unexpectedly, out of the Islamic world. This wonderous and beautiful creation is known as *The Rubáiyát of Omar Khayyam*.

Omar Khayyam, (1050 – 1122) whose surname means "the tentmaker", was a Persian mathematician and astronomer attached to the royal court of Neyshabur. He was, in fact, the foremost mathematician of his time and along with other scientists reformed the Persian calendar. He is most famous, however, as the author of the *Rubáiyat,* a series of about 1,000 four-line stanzas reflecting on nature, love and humanity.

It was the English poet and translator Edward Fitzgerald[2] who, in 1859, introduced Omar Khayyam to the Western world with his translation of 100 quatrains. Fitzgerald was wise enough not to attempt a literal translation of Omar's words, which would have been clumsy and unattractive. Instead he rewrote each quatrain in his own words in an attempt to capture the essence of the original in a poetic and elegant way. This author personally considers it a great and joyous success, and that *The Rubáiyát of Omar Khayyam* ought to be considered as something quite close in concept to a Dionysian's "Bible". Here are a few verses:

VII

Come fill the cup, and in the fire of spring
The winter garment of repentance fling:
The bird of time has but a little way
To fly – and lo! The bird is on the wing

XXVI

Oh, come with old Khayyam and leave the wise
To talk; one thing is certain, that life flies;
One thing is certain, and the rest is lies;
The flower that once has blown forever dies.

XXXIX

How long, how long, in infinite pursuit
Of this and that endeavour and dispute?
Better be merry with the fruitful grape
Than sadden after none, or bitter fruit.

LI

The moving finger writes: and having writ,
Moves on: nor all thy piety nor wit
Shall lure it back to cancel half a line,
Nor all thy tears wash out a word of it.

LXXI

And much as wine has played the infidel,
And robbed me of my robe of honour – well,
I often wonder what the vintners buy
One half so precious as the goods they sell.

One of the strangest places to find The Spirit of Dionysos thriving, through *entheos* and *ekstasis,* is within Islam itself. The two main schools of Islam are the Sunni and Shi'ite sects, which Christians might consider analogous to Catholic and Protestant, but there is a third. This is the mysterious and mystical Sufi.

Very little is know about Sufism before the 10th century, from where the earliest extant documents come, but we do know that many of Sufism's rituals and doctrine are very similar (occasionally identical) to earlier mystical movements established in the regions where Sufism first arose. These would include Eastern Christianity, Gnosticism, Neo-Platonism, Manicheanism and Buddhism.

Sufis believe that it is possible to attain direct knowledge of and spiritual union with God, in European terms called *gnosis*, through various methods such as listening to music and poetry, humour, dancing and other methods. Much of the poetry and song symbolises divine love and ecstasy via the Islamic taboo subjects of sexual love and alcoholic intoxication.

Sufism has often and quite regularly had problems with more orthodox types of Islam, too. In offering gnosis they also offer a threatening alternative to the Apolline tradition of Koran-based scholarship and subservience to the Imams, which has made traditionalists very suspicious and seen Sufis accused of placing themselves outside Shari'ah law. In response, and in order to protect themselves, various Sufi groups have either gone underground and become obscure and secretive or else have cultivated an image of utter zealotry, and taken a highly active part in militant Jihad action against neighbouring infidel states.

Violence apart, one of the Sufi's best known and most loved methods leading towards gnosis is through humour. One popular character in their humorous stories is the sage, Nasrudin who we could see as something like the Brer Rabbit of Islamic humour. Following is a story[3] I stole from Robert Anton Wilson, which describes Nasruddin beautifully:

The venerable sage, Mullah Nasruddin was once condemned to death for ceratin witty and satirical sayings that disturbed the local Shah. Nasruddin immediately offered a bargain: "Postpone the execution one year," he implored the Shah, "and I will teach your horse to fly." Intrigued by this, the Shah agreed.

One day thereafter, a friend asked Nasruddin if he really expected to escape death by this manoeuvre.

"Why not?" answered the divine Mullah. "A lot can happen in a year. There might be a revolution and a new government. There might be a foreign invasion and we'd all be living under a new Shah. Then again, the present Shah might die of natural causes, or somebody in the palace might poison him. As you know it's traditional for a new Shah to pardon all condemned criminals awaiting execution when he takes the throne. Besides that, during the year my captors will have many opportunities for carelessness and I will always be looking for an opportunity to escape.

"And finally, " Nasruddin concluded, "if the worst comes to the worst, maybe I **can** teach that damned horse to fly!"

Dionysos Across the Millennium

History and geography gravitate inexorably towards the here and now. The readers of this work are expected to be English-speaking people of the 21st century. This does not intended to discourage anybody else who wishes to read it of course, but I believe that the vast majority of the readership will be living in a time and culture no more than a generation or two from the events and characters in this section. This is no longer the Dionysian current in mythology and history. This is where the Dionysian current has brought us now, and this is how and through whom it affects the lives we lead today.

Hippies

The birth of the truly modern Dionysian current can arguably be placed in mid/late 1960's San Francisco, in what very quickly became known as the Hippy movement. While the Beatniks had the first true subculture, the hippies created what was to become the most famous and first truly international subculture, and the first with a meaningful philosophy beyond the simple commonalities of music and fashion. The rise of international mass media, especially television, had an exceptionally powerful effect here.

The Hippy movement espoused what were at the time some extremely radical views and ideals: pacifism in the face of the Vietnam conflict; non-violent passive resistance to authoritarian rule; the study of Eastern religious practises and the use of psychotropic substances; organic foods; communal living and, of course, "free love".

Hippies went out of fashion for a while, but their ideals in radical left-wing culture have never really gone away. They resurface regularly as the driving force behind many different modern activisms and subcultures, such as modern environmentalism, the animal rights and vegan movements, the "Occupy" anti-capitalist movement and the love and sex idealism of Polyamory.

Ken Kesey

Obviously, the hippies did not simply spring from nowhere. The roots of the Hippy movement can be traced directly back to the drug and lifestyle experimenters of the 1950's that we met earlier, such as Burroughs, Ginsberg and Kerouac. One of the founding fathers of the Hippy movement was the novelist and friend of the Beatniks, the remarkable Ken Kesey.

Kesey was born in Colorado, US, in 1935 to a farming family and gained a solid but not unusual education, acquiring a degree in journalism (speech and communication) in 1957 and studying creative writing at Stanford the next year. It was while studying at Stanford that he began the first very drafts of his most famous novel, *One Flew Over the Cuckoo's Nest*.

Ironically, it was the establishment which turned Kesey into an anti-establishment icon. In 1959 the CIA began secretly testing psychoactive drugs on volunteers in an attempt to discover whether they could be used for mind-control purposes[1]. Kesey was one of those volunteers and the experiences he had, as well as his experience of working as an orderly in a mental hospital, allowed him to complete *Cuckoo's Nest*. The novel was an immediate success and, using the money from that and the sale of his place at Stanford, he moved to California where he began his famous *Acid-Test* parties. These parties, noted in novel and poem by Alan Ginsberg, Tom Wolfe and Hunter S Thompson, involved music, strobe lighting, psychedelic decor and artwork and, of course, LSD.

Kesey's greatest influence on the Hippy movement came when he decided to take his party on the road. In 1964 Kesey and a group of friends, calling themselves *The Merry Pranksters,* acquired an old school bus which they painted up in wild psychedelic colours and patterns and named *Furthur* (sic). They persuaded Neal Cassady (the inspiration for *Dean Moriarty* from Kerouac's *On The Road*) to drive it and travelled across America from California all the way to New York taking with them a philosophy of fun and experimentation, and happily handing out LSD (which was still legal at the time) to anyone who wanted it. On the way they paid visits to their friends and heroes, Jack Kerouac, Alan Ginsberg and Timothy Leary. The story of their journey is related particularly well by Tom Wolfe in his 1968 "non-fiction" novel, *The Electric Kool-Aid Acid Test*. *Kool-Aid* is a dried and powdered American soft drink which is reconstituted by mixing with water and sugar. The *Electric* version is, of course, laced with LSD.

Further Acid Tests followed in various locations until Kesey's arrest for possession of marijuana in 1965. He fled to Mexico for 8 months and was sentenced to 5 months jail on his return to the States. After that Kesey moved into his parents' farm in Oregon and lived a somewhat quieter life. He still wrote and promoted his ideals of love and psychedelic drug use as tools for consciousness expansion[2], but left most of the actual activism to the rest of the Merry Pranksters – although he did make an appearance at Woodstock.

Kesey died of surgical complications after a liver operation in 2001, at the age of 66. He knew very well how strong his own influence and the influence of the Hippy movement had been on modern culture and was quoted in an interview on Tom Snyder's television programme, The Tomorrow Show (in reference to the 1960's and psychedelic experimentation) that:

"It was the beginning of a real true revolution that is still going on"

Timothy Leary

Timothy Leary is possibly the most widely known personality from the Hippy period that was not a rock star. Nor was he a great poet or radical novelist. He was, in fact, a psychologist.

Leary was born in 1920 and lived a relatively straightforward and succesful life for his first 40 years or so. He grew up in Massachusets and attended college and university in also in Massachusets, and in Alabama and Berkely, California. He gained his PhD in psychology at the age of 30 and eventually became a lecturer in psychology at Harvard from 1959 until 1963.

While succesful, his was not an entirely happy life and around the time of his first wife's suicide in 1955 Leary described himself as *an anonymous institutional employee who drove to work each morning in a long line of commuter cars and drove home each night and drank martinis ... like several million middle-class, liberal, intellectual robots.*[1]

Leary completely altered the course of his life through the discovery of psilocybin mushrooms, which he took on a trip to Mexico with a friend who had experimented with them previously. He later commented that he had learned more about his mind in those few hours than in fifteen years of pychological research. He was also inspired to study the effects of hallucinogenic substances and began a study at Harvard using a synthesised psilocybin substitute on criminals and alcoholics as an aid to their recovery and rehabilitation[2]. It did appear very successful, with only a 20% rate of backsliding amongst the criminals, as opposed to the usual rate of 60%.

Unfortunately it was not long afterwards that the Drug Enforcement Agency declared psilocybin illegal and no further studies were carried out. Under Leary's tutelage and care many of his friends, particulary University professors, philosophers and graduate students, took LSD and psilocybin. Almost universally they reported such marvellous events as mystical visions, spiritual awakenings and very positive permanent changes to their lives.

In a failed attempt to keep LSD legal in the USA, in 1966 Leary created the League of Spiritual Discovery the aim of which was to use the protections of religious freedom to allow the use of hallucinogens. It did not work, but it did tune into the zeitgeist of the time. Furthermore it earned him an invitation to the *Human Be-In* in San Francisco's Golden Gate Park in January 1967, where the Hippy movement can be said to have officially begun and where he first quoted his famous phrase, *"Turn on, tune in drop out!"*

Leary also collaborated with the writer Brain Barret, and did a large amount of work with another Dionysian hero whom we will look at in more detail later, the remarkable Robert Anton Wilson. One of their joint efforts produced a radical map of the human mind called the *Seven Circuits of Consciousness* (to which an eighth was later added), with descriptions of what these "circuits" do. The first four are the normal patterns of behaviour activated by genetics and upbringing, the others are described as evolutionary offshoots leading to greater enlightenment, self-awareness and cosmic experience which are accessible via various exercises and the use of certain mind-altering substances.

Inevitably trouble with the authorities, arrest and imprisonment were to affect Leary. Amazingly by modern standards, he was sentenced to 30 years imprisonment, a $30,000 fine and forced psychiatric treatment for marijuana possession in 1965, which he eventually appealed successfully against. He was arrested again in 1968 on the same charge and sentenced to 10 years with a further 10 years for the 1965 arrest. Whilst in prison he was subjected to psychological tests, ironically many of which he had designed himself and could therefore "cheat" quite easily, making himself out to be a quiet and "normal" person. The tests got him a very low-security placing from which he escaped in September 1970 and the radical group, The Weather Underground smuggled him and his then wife, Rosemary to Algeria.

He travelled later to Switzerland, where he and Rosemary split, and then onwards to Vienna and Beirut. The U.S. authorities eventually caught up with him in Afghanistan in 1973 and Richard Nixon's "most dangerous man in America" was placed in solitary confinement because, as the judge at his trial said, "If he is allowed to travel freely, he will speak publicly and spread his ideas". Facing 95 years incarceration, Leary spent much of his time writing and developing his futurist and trahshumanist ideas.

Eventually America saw sense and Californian governor, Jerry Brown released Leary in 1976. He then spent his last twenty years writing, lecturing and attempting to become the most famous psychologist on the planet. He may well have succeeded.

Leary never stood still and was constantly developing both his ideas and his friendships, and integrating new concepts, such as the internet which he described as the "LSD of the 1990's" describing its potential for the expansion of human consciousness. He became friends with such famous and exceptional individuals as William Gibson, Johnny Depp, Susan Sarandon and the musician and producer, John Frusciante. He even had his own acting career and took part in (amongst other things) John Lennon and Yoko Ono's recording of *Give Peace a Chance*.

Leary died in 1996, aged 75 years, of inoperable prostate cancer. Even terminal illness did not truly stop him and he spent much of his remaining months discussing and lecturing via the internet on such subjects as drugs, transhumanism, futurism, space migration and embracing death. His last moments were videotaped at his request, his final words being "Why not?" several times in a variety of intonations and finally "beautiful".

As a psychologist Timothy Leary had an influence as important as Freud or Jung - albeit less well known - but it is as a figure of popular culture he became best known and, perhaps most effective. He has even had a film, *Timothy Leary's Dead*, specifically made in his honour. He has inspired, collaborated with and been the subject matter of film makers, artists, writers and, especially, musicians. He has worked with John Lennon, Devo, Ash Ra Tempel and appeared in a variety of pop videos and films. Most recently he was mentioned in the excellent and inspiring film, *The Men Who Stare at Goats*, in which one character believes he saw him in a vision and another replies "Timothy Leary's dead"!

Dead Pop Stars

It has been said earlier and often in this book that Dionysos and Apollo need each other. The wholly Apolline society becomes rigid, totalitarian and ossified while the totally Dionysian becomes dissolute and self-destructive. Much the same can be said of human beings. The undiluted Dionysian lifestyle has one commonly recurring feature, its shortness.

The late 1960s and early 70s saw the meteoric rise and sudden crash of a number of musical geniuses who, like their spiritual forebears the Romantic poets of the late 18th century, took the Dionysian life to an extreme beyond which their bodies could cope. Amongst them we find Brian Jones, Jimi Hendrix, Janis Joplin and, of course, Jim Morrison – people who seemingly began a pattern which continues to the present day. Fascinatingly, these four individuals not only lived and performed at the same time and in the same medium, they also lived for the same length of time. All four died at the age of 27.[1]

By virtue of his birthday, the first of our little band of human meteors is the Rolling Stones' guitarist and leading light, Brian Jones. Jones was born on the 28th February 1942 and died on the 3rd July 1969, making him our shortest-lived subject at 27 years and 4 months.

Jones wasn't just a guitarist, he was also the manager and the driving force behind the Stones during their early years, and an extremely talented multi-instrumentalist. He also played, amongst other things, clarinet, dulcimer, sitar, marimba and mellotron. In fact, by the late 1960's he was known as much for his experimental approach to music as his guitar playing.

Unfortunately he could not function well as a gestalt team member, which was the manner in which the Stones were evolving as a group. His earlier role had been much more prominent as a personality and so as the limelight slowly passed to other members, particularly Mick Jagger and Keith Richards, he began to feel alienated. He usually travelled separately from the rest of the band, and when managing as well as playing he earned more money which caused a certain amount of resentment. The alienation also led Jones to seek solace in quite a large range of narcotics. His dependence on them made him unwell, extremely unpredictable and often quite anti-social.

After being refused a work permit due to previous drug convictions, which would have allowed him to tour America with the Stones, Jones was asked to leave the band. A few weeks later he was found face-down at the bottom of his swimming pool. There were rumours which came to nothing that he was murdered by a disgruntled builder, but the official verdict was misadventure.

It's Jones' legend which makes him a Dionysian as much as his intense, flamboyant and ultimately self-destructive lifestyle. He was naturally rebellious, anti-authoritarian and loved fame. His early death did nothing but increase that reputation, to the extent that his body had to be buried 12 feet deep to deter souvenir hunters.

Our second member, and longest-lived at 27 years and almost 10 months, is the remakable and unique guitarist, Jimi Hendrix.

Johnny Allen Hendrix (whose name was later changed to James Marshall Hendrix) was born in Seattle, USA on the 27th November 1942. Growing up with his parents and siblings he suffered from great physical and financial hardships, sometimes living with his grandmother to escape the instability of his home life. He acquired his first guitar at the age of 15 and this appeared to completely change his fortunes. He taught himself to play by watching guitarists, listening to records and asking tips from other players. That and constant practise began to turn the shy, sensitive boy into the wild and flamboyant rock god he became.

Guitar music seems to have been just about the only thing Hendrix was any good at. He was a mediocre school student at best, and when forced to join the army to avoid a jail sentence[2] he was considered lazy, completely undisciplined and a hopeless shot. His short military stint did have one fortunate result in that he met his friend and future bass player, Billy Cox while stationed at Fort Campbell.

Hendrix also appears to have had a healthy disrespect for the mass media. He regularly lied to newspapers about his past telling them, for instance, that he was expelled from High School on racist grounds and that he got his discharge from the army by pretending to be homosexual. The most famous example of his relaxed attitude to responsibilty and authority is most definitely his appearance on the *Lulu Show* in 1969 where he "suddenly decided" to stop playing *Hey Joe* part way through and instead played *Sunshine of Your Love* in honour of the recently disbanded group, Cream. As this was a completely live broadcast there was not very much that could be done, but the producer pulled his plug out when he clashed with Lulu's final song.

Before Hendrix the electric guitar was little more than an amplified version of an acoustic one. After Hendrix it became something completely new and different. He pioneered playing techniques that had rarely, if ever, been heard and he used new and innovative electronics to great effect including the fuzz pedal, wah-

wah pedal, other pedals designed specifically for him, and deliberate feedback.

Hendrix's death came in September 1970 after a party in London's Notting Hill. It seems that he drank a great deal of wine and then mistakenly took an overdose of his girlfriend's sleeping tablets. Ironically, it was the wine which killed him when he choked on his own vomit whilst sleeping. He left almost 300 unreleased recordings.

Janis Joplin, the only woman in our little gang-of-four, was at least as powerful and original a musician as her male counterparts in the masculine-dominated world of 1960's music, and has been justly lauded as such.

An attention-seeking child, she was born in Port Arthur, Texas on 19th January 1943. While her parents were respectable, lower-middle class people, Joplin herself felt more at home with outcasts and oddities. She was a misfit at school, being what we would nowadays consider "nerdy". She preferred reading and painting to the usual and expected teenage social activities, she was overweight and also cursed with acne bad enough to leave scars.

Her singing career began in her church choir, but some of her friends had blues albums and listening to these is what prompted her into professional performance. She made her first amateur recording in 1962 with her own song, *What Good Can Drinkin' Do?* which seems strangely appropriate in hindsight.

Not long afterwards she moved from Texas to San Francisco, and this is where her on-off love affair with narcotics really began to take hold. She became known as a speed-freak, experimented with heroin as well as the usual psychedelics and, of course, drank heavily. Her particular favourite tipple was reputed to be Southern Comfort. During the mid 60's friends attempted to rescue her from her various drug habits, which had turned a chubby girl into a walking skeleton, by sending her back home. It worked for a while and Joplin cleaned up her act, enrolled at college and started to dress a little more modestly whilst still supporting herself by singing.

Pretty soon, though, she was spotted and poached by the band, *Big Brother and the Holding Company* and was back in San Fransisco by mid 1966. She took to the road and studio with them and even managed to stay away from hard drugs for a few months. From this point onwards Joplin's career as a singer went meteoric. She was decribed by Laurie Jacobson in *Hollywood Heatbreak* as, "the most staggering leading woman in rock... she slinks like tar, scowls like war... clutching the knees of a final stanza, begging it not to leave"[3]

Perhaps it was the intensity of the workload or just her own natural tendency to self-abuse but by 1969 Joplin was massively addicted to heroin again, to the point where it was seriously affecting her performances. Friends attempted to keep her clean and, once more, she completely gave up drugs and alcohol for a while when on an extended holiday with a friend in Brazil. When she returned to the US, though, the cycle began again and eventually it killed her. She died on the floor of a Los Angeles hotel room on 4th October 1970.

The sheer intensity of Joplin's singing seemed to match the chaotic intensity of her whole life and it would not be unfair to say that her early death was almost inevitable. Her influence, though, far outweighs her four short years of fame. She has had a stage play made about her life and has been given a huge amount of posthumous awards She has been cited as the basis for the main character in the film, *The Rose* and has even been considered a major player in making tattoos acceptable for women.

The last of our little bunch of self-destructive rock stars has something of a superior position over the other three. They lived a Dionysian lifestyle but he actually was Dionysos himself, or so some people have claimed. He was, of course, Jim Morrison lead singer of the American rock band, The Doors.

In many ways Morrison is more myth than man, a status he himself enjoyed and cultivated. Oliver Stone's superb 1991 film, *The Doors* captures this mythology beautifully. Although members of the band have complained that many episodes in the film are pure fiction, Morrison himself would almost certainly have loved it.

The cult which has grown up around him has given him an almost god-like status in the eyes of many of his admirers, and in many ways that is quite fitting. Morrison himself could not bear to be ordinary and thrived on the adoration of his fans while, paradoxically, suffering from the increasing pressures fame brought to him. Even the fact of his death has been questioned and some people really believe that Jim is still out there somewhere.

The child destined to become Jim Morrison was born James Douglas Morrison on the 8th December 1943 in Florida. Due to his father being a high-ranking member of the US Navy, the family moved around a lot and the young Morrison was brought up in many different towns and states across the USA. He had the good fortune to be adaptable and extremely clever, with a reported IQ of 149, so it did not affect his education too much. He managed to graduate well from high school, attend college and eventually moved to Los Angeles, to attend UCLA and study for a degree in film making which he acquired in 1965.

One of the young Morrison's formative experiences, and another story which has become legendary in the retelling, happened when he was four years old. The Morrison family drove past a road accident involving a family of Native Americans. That basic fact was certainly true, but over the years Morrison built it into a scene of death and carnage on a desert highway and an experience involving the spirits of the dead Indians. Arguably, in his own mind this became truer than the event itself, especially considering that he was only four years old at the time, and thus became extremely influential over his self-image and the image he tried to project on stage and screen. He referred to the event several times in songs and poems such as *Ghost Song* and *Dawn's Highway*.

Just as Dionysos needs Apollo, Morrison needed someone sensible and clear-headed to balance him. Without Ray Manzerak and the two other members of the Doors, Morrison would most likely have become an intellectual, poetic beach bum and disappeared into obscurity. The Doors gave him structure and solidity, he gave them fire, snakes, visions and, above all, fame!

Morrison met Manzerak, keyboard player and a fellow UCLA

student, in Venice Beach, California and between them they found drummer, John Densmore. The line-up was completed by Densmore's recommendation, Robbie Krieger on guitar. They took their name from Aldous Huxley's novel about LSD, *The Doors of Perception* which takes its name in turn from William Blake. By 1966 they were opening for Van Morrison, someone Jim Morrison greatly admired and from whom he learned much of his stagecraft.

Another legendary episode, but this time with documentary evidence, happened on the extremely important Ed Sullivan show in 1967. By way of a simplified explanation, if you were in a band in America in the 1960s and you got onto *Sullivan*, you had "made it". The story goes that *Light My Fire*, written by Krieger, was number one in the American charts and the band had been asked to play it, but with one proviso: the lyric "girl we couldn't get much higher" sounded too drug-related and could the band change it to "girl we couldn't get much better"? Obviously Morrison sang the original words, claiming later to have simply forgotten. That is eminently possible, of course, except that the same line comes both at the beginning and end of the song. Either way it all added to the legend, and got them banned from doing the show again. Morrison didn't care though because, "We already did".

The career of The Doors went from strength to strength over the next few years. Morrison's personal life, however, became ever more chaotic. He had a long-term partner in Pamela Courson but affairs and one-night stands with a huge number of other women including Nico, Grace Slick, Janis Joplin (allegedly), several fans and most famously, the author and journalist Patricia Kennealy. Kennealy was a Pagan and she and Morrison were handfasted (a Pagan wedding) in 1970, although there were obviously no legal papers to proclaim them married.

It's unlikely that Morrison took the handfasting seriously. He was a notoriously heavy drinker and experimenter with narcotics and was arrested several times for drunkenness, lewd behaviour and similar offences. By 1969 he was regularly turning up to stage shows and recording sessions late and usually drunk. Many people have referred to this as his "Elvis phase" and he did indeed gain a great deal of weight through drinking and self-indulgence. He also grew a beard and swapped his previously iconic leather trousers and jacket for t-shirts and jeans. It is possible that he was attempting to distance himself from his most famous image, as shown in the extremely well-known black and white photographs of the "Young Lion" taken by Joel Brodsky in 1967.

Morrison and Courson moved to Paris in early 1971, primarily to escape regular threats of arrest and the pressures of fame. While this move did not stop Morrison's drinking he did seem to become happier and more relaxed in Paris. He lost weight, shaved off his beard and would take long walks around the city admiring the architecture. On the 3rd July 1971 Courson found him dead in the bathtub. The official cause of death was given by the French coroner as "heart failure".

Morrison's death is just as legendary as his life and the source of a great deal of debate. The doctor who examined his body did not perform an autopsy because it was unnecessary under French law where there appeared to be no foul play. Several theories have come about, many based on the conflicting reports given by Courson herself, such as his accidental snorting of heroin believing it to be cocaine, or that he had developed asthma and had been coughing up blood for some months. It was even suggested for a while that his death was a cover-up which led to a great deal of distress for his family and friends who were hounded by "Jim hunters". The most recent theory has stated that he actually died of a heroin overdose on a nightclub toilet and his body was taken back to his apartment by the two drug dealers who sold him the heroin. The simplest story is probably the most likely, that self-abuse eventually wore him out and his heart gave in, but that hardly matters where the legend is concerned[4]. Unfortunately the only real witness, Pamela Courson died herself three years later of a heroin overdose. She was also 27 years old.

Jim Morrison wasn't just the singer in a band. He was a lyricist; a poet and a fan particularly of Rimbaud; a film maker and actor in his own films and, ultimately, the iconic rebel rock star. He had a deep and abiding interest in Native American spirituality, mysticism and shamanism. Many compared him to Dionysos himself and legend says that he often referred to himself in Neitzschean terms as Dionysos and to Manzerak as Apollo. There is no real confirmation of this, although Morrison and the whole band were extremely intelligent and well-read individuals so there is also no reason why they wouldn't have recognised and applied the archetypes to themselves.True or not, it fits the legend perfectly.

New York in Velvet

While Morrison and friends were still at college a new movement in art was growing on the other side of the country in New York. This was the movement which became known as Pop Art and New York was the home of its most famous exponent, Andy Warhol.

It is difficult to describe the Pop Art movement or even Warhol himself as truly Dionysian in nature. Whilst Pop Art was radical inasmuch as it was new in the early 1960s, it was not truly radical or challenging in its nature. Pop Art celebrated the popular, mundane and mass-produced. Warhol's famous multiple images of *Marilyn Monroe* and *Campbells Soup Tins* illustrate and define this attitude perfectly.

Warhol himself was a strange and complicated man. He appears to have been a very kindly person who often volunteered at homeless shelters. He was a devout Roman Catholic but he was also homosexual, and over the years produced a great many homo-erotic photographs. Even so, it is thought that he was also a virgin for his whole life. He was exceptionally obsessive and catalogued souvenirs of his life in the most minute of detail, yet he employed other people to help create many of his paintings and films. He began his career as a purely commercial artist, earning his living by illustrating magazines and did not take on his radical mantle until the opening of *The Factory* in 1962, at the relatively advanced age of 34.

The Factory was Warhol's New York studio and he filled it with New York's most remarkable bohemians. Many of them practically lived in the studio, experimenting with drugs and sex, and consequently starring in several of his films. Warhol called these people his "Superstars", and they included such individuals as the actor, Joe Dallesandro, the tragic heiress, Edie Sedgwick, and the transgendered actress, Candy Darling. It is as a film maker that Warhol can be seen at his most radical and shocking. He used graphic nudity, sex and drug-taking as the majority of his material, and it was not uncommon for showings of his films to be raided and closed down by the police.

The heyday of The Factory lasted for about 6 years at the studio on East 47th Street in Manhattan, although Warhol also called his subsequent studios The Factory. It was often referred to as the Silver Factory after it was decorated with tinfoil and silver paint by the in-house photographer, Billy Name who also found the red couch used in many of Warhol's early films.

The dream, as dreams often do, went somewhat sour when Warhol was shot by one of his minor protogés, Valerie Solanas, in 1968[1]. Fortunately he survived but the experience made him much more careful and controlling about who he worked with and invited to The Factory. It also made him ill and scared for the rest of his life and, for many, the Andy Warhol they knew and loved had died inside. He eventually died for real in 1987 at the age of 58, in his sleep after a gall bladder operation.

The Factory was rather more than just a place for the production of the purely visual arts, there was also music. During the mid 60s Warhol took a group of musicians under his wing, allowing them to rehearse at The Factory and designing their album sleeves, as well as featuring them in some of his films and even becoming their manager. They were, of course, the *Velvet Underground.*

Often described as proto-punk, the combination of experimental sounds and often disturbing lyrical content produced by Lou Reed, John Cale and Maureen Tucker, amongst a few others, has been cited as a powerful influence by many modern and radical musicians ever since. Many of their songs can also be seen as a commentary of the life and times of The Factory and the people involved in it. Such songs as *Heroin* and the dark Sado-Masochistic fantasy, *Venus In Furs* speak volumes about their interests and attitudes at that time and place. Lou Reed's 1972 solo song, *Walk on the Wild Side* is a history lesson which features real people from The Factory.

The *Holly* who *came from Miami FLA* is the transvestite actress, Holly Woodlawn; *Candy* who *came out from the island* was the transexual actress, Candy Darling; *Little Joe* who *never once gave it away* is Joe Dallesandro; the *Sugar Plum Fairy* was Joe Campbell and *Jackie* who was *just speeding away* was another transvestite actress, Jackie Curtis. At the time of writing only Dallesandro and Woodlawn still survive. All of these individuals can be seen in a variety of Warhol's films.

In 1966 Warhol created a series of multi-media events called the *Exploding Plastic Inevitable* for which the Velvet Underground provided the music. For these events Warhol also introduced them to one of their best and most famous collaborators, and a fascinating Dionysian in her own right, Nico.

The Rise, Fall and Rise of Nico

In her short life of 49 years the remarkable Nico worked her way from obscurity to fame and back again twice over. She sustained careers as a model, actress, singer and composer as well as a lifestyle of almost constant international travel and a long period of heroin addiction, and managed to combine this with many relationships and an attempt at parenthood. She became a musician despite being partially deaf, and spoke five (some say seven) languages despite leaving school at only 13 years old.

Christa Päffgen was born in October 1938 in Nazi-controlled Cologne, Germany. The family moved soon afterwards to the small town of Spreewald, near Berlin where she was brought up by her mother and grandparents. Her father died in a concentration camp, but otherwise little is known about her family circumstances. The war finished when Christa was 6, and her mother fled the Russian occupation of Germany by moving to the American sector of Berlin, which was pretty much in ruins by that time.

At the age of 13 Christa left school to work in a lingerie shop which is where her fame began. She was a very striking girl, unusually tall at 5'10", blonde with strong square features and pale, clear skin. Fashion insiders noticed her and within a year her mother had taken her to Berlin to work as a fashion model. She received her new name in 1954 when she was sent on a modelling contract to Ibiza at the age of 15. The photographer nicknamed her Nico after his ex-boyfriend[1], and very soon the young Nico was jetting all over the world as a top international model.

Her first work as an actress came in 1958 in television commercials and a small part in a film called *La Tempesta*. In 1959 Frederico Fellini spotted her hanging about in Rome on the set where he was filming *La Dolce Vita* and gave her a small role on the spot. After that she moved to New York to take acting lessons which she funded by modelling.

In Paris a few years later Nico acquired her first substantial role in the 1962 film, *Strip-Tease* and also recorded the theme song with Serge Gainsburgh, although a different version was used in the film. In 1962 she also gave birth to her only child, Christian Aaron[2]. Although he has denied paternity the father is reputed to be the French actor, Alain Delon. Due to her unreliable jet-set lifestyle Nico was not able to be a devoted mother to her son so the boy was looked after, and eventually adopted, by Delon's parents.

In 1965 she met Brian Jones of the Rolling Stones who helped her produce her first official record, *I'm Not Sayin'*. As sales went it was not especially succesful but it did mark her first appearance as a singer in her own right. Following that she met, and began working with, Andy Warhol. He put her in a few of his films, *Chelsea Girls* being the most famous, and introduced her to the Velvet Underground. Her low, flat and almost stereotyped Germanic style worked well with the Velvet Underground's experimental approach and she sang with them on four songs, most notably the extremely famous *All Tomorrow's Parties*.

It was not an easy relationship, though. Nico was, apparently, quite a strong and confrontational person and her partial deafness occasionally led her to sing off key, for which she was derided. Nonetheless, she formed a good partnership with the band's violinist and founder member, John Cale. He helped to produce her work and played on several of her future solo albums during the late 1960s. Nico had taught herself to play the harmonium by this time and was also writing many of the songs herself.

Between 1969 and 1979 she made several relatively unsuccesful films with her lover, Phillipe Garrel, and due to a number of arguments she was dropped by her record label. To put it bluntly, Nico spent all of the 1970s completely down at heel in New York and London. There is, of course, every chance that she had simply become unfashionable. She had a band and still toured but without any great interest. Her heavy smoking and drinking also had their effects as did her heroin habit, and it was not until the 1980s that she managed to get her act back together again.

She made her comeback with a concert in 1980 at CBGB in New York, which received glowing reviews. Nico's star was again ascending and it is fairly certain that her camp status as a 60s icon helped a lot. She made two more studio albums, both in collaboration with John Cale and many of her live performances were recorded during successful tours of Europe and the Far East.

By 1988, at the age of 49, Nico had cleaned up her act. She was living mostly in London and Manchester[3], had managed to break her heroin addiction and taken on a healthy eating and exercise regime. During a holiday on Ibiza with her son in July of that year she had some kind of attack and fell unconscious from her bicycle. She later died in hospital of a brain haemmorhage. Her body is buried with her mother's in Berlin.

Nico might have ended up as just another anonymous face on the cover of Vogue but for her remarkable strength and, to large extent, self-centredness. She decided that she wanted to do something and then damn well did it, despite the difficulties which stood in her way. Some considered that it was because she hated her own beauty and was bored with the ordinariness of life. This might be the case. She certainly spent most of her adult life experimenting with new forms in film and music whilst still remaining true to herself. Consequently, while never having achieved the massive popularity of, say, the Doors or the Rolling Stones she has still had an incredibly wide influence, especially on women in music and on such radical musical movements as Punk and Goth. Nico's friends and ex-lovers (of which there were many) produced tribute concerts in London and Berlin during 2008, to celebrate what would have been her 70th birthday.

RAW

For many the Hippy period can be said to have ended at the Altamont festival in 1969. Woodstock had happened beautifully in northern New York state during the previous August and there were various attempts to reproduce the Woodstock spirit across America. Altamont was a free festival held on December 6th in northern California. It was organised by members of Ken Kesey's favourite band, *The Grateful Dead* who alledgedly hired Hells Angels as security. The Angels had often often taken the job at previous events without any trouble at all, but this time something went wrong.

Although peaceful to begin with, the large amount of people and the erroneously perceived "us and them" attitude of the bands and the Hell's Angels eventually took its toll. The crowd was acting aggressively, there was no barrier between the stage and the forward-pressing crowd and everyone had been drinking all day. Bottles were thrown at bands. Perfomers and Hell's Angels were attacked and fights broke out amongst the crowd. During the set by the Rolling Stones a young fan, Meredith Hunter, attempted to climb onto the stage and the Angels violently threw him back. He became enraged and took a gun from his pocket, at which point one of the Angels panicked, produced a knife and stabbed him to death.[1]

All this pretty much sounded the death knell for the idealised, peaceful and loving Hippy dream. In many respects Hippydom would have faded away anyway, as all youth movements do eventually. There was something more to it, though, than simply a youthful fashion and many of the aspects and ideals espoused during the hippy movement, such as free love, consciousness expansion, and peaceful anarchism, were held, developed and pushed forward by some great Dionysian spirits, especially in occult and mystical circles. One of the greatest of these was Robert Anton Wilson, the philosopher, novelist, futurist, polymath, civil libertarian and Discordian mystic sometimes known as *RAW*.

Robert Edward Wilson (he adopted the name Anton later) was born in Brooklyn, New York in January 1932 and grew up in a variety of towns in New York state. He suffered from polio as a child which he generally dealt with very well, except for the occasional need for a walking stick, until quite an advanced age. He acquired a decent education at Catholic Grammar school and Brooklyn Technical High School and later at New York University where he studied engineering and mathematics at New York University while working as an ambulance driver.

Wilson's adult life was not the easiest experience that it could have been. He married the poet Arlen Riley in 1958 and they had four children. One of their daughters was gang-raped in 1971 and their youngest, Patricia known as Luna, was beaten to death in a store robbery at the age of 15. In such circumstances many parents would simply have given up on the human race and on living, but Wilson simply could not do that. An extended quote from his essay, *Ten Good Reasons to Get Out of Bed in the Morning* explains it beautifully:

I believe that I have as good a reason as anyone to be depressed. Besides my personal misfortunes, I have been visiting prisons for three years now, and I know the horrors of what our society looks like from the very bottom, from the black holes of isolation cells where men are chained like beasts. Twenty years ago I worked as an ambulance attendant in Harlem, and I saw what poverty and racism can do at their worst. Nobody needs to teach me about the inhumanity of *humanity*. *Yet I still believe there is, as the Sufis say, a divinty within each person that can be released if love and faith and optimism can be released.*[2]

Wilson did a lot of odd jobs until he finally came into his own as a writer when he got the job of Editor on Playboy magazine fron 1965 to 1971. In 1975 he published what is probably his most famous work, in collaboration with his fellow novelist and Playboy co-worker Robert Shea, *The Illuminatus! Trilogy*.

Illuminatus! is a huge and bizarre work, once described as a fairy tale for paranoids. It covers conspiracy theories, sex, mysticism, aliens, Atlantis, anarchism, history, counterculture, Discordianism and even gave us the wonderful word, *Fnord*, the meaning of which it would be most apprpriate to leave to the reader to discover. It has also been turned into a role-playing game and a stage play. What is most remarkable about *Illuminatus!* is that it is so complex and rich, without any specific bias or viewpoint, that it can be used by just about anyone to demonstrate the validity of just about anything, or as it is known in the book, *Operation Mindfuck*. This wonderful quality of non-defintion has made it something akin to a Bible for modern Chaos magickians and lovers of conspiracy theory.

In his years of writing Wilson has produced 35 books, both fiction and non-fiction, although the distinction is often somewhat blurred, and well over 1,000 articles. On top of all this, and in addition to his and Arlen's creation of the *Institute for the Study of the Human Future*, his long-term friendship with Timothy Leary led him to create the *Starflight Network* and join the *Association for Consciousness Exploration* in order to develop and promulgate his ideas. He was also a member of the Church of the Subgenius, known as Pope Bob, a campaigner against "the war on certain drugs" and a promoter of jury nullification, which allows juries to remove a law they consider unjust. One of his most famous ideas is known as *Maybe Logic*, which proposes to remove all words of absolute certainty, such as "is", from language, thus making any form of religious or political fundamentalism impossible. If all anybody can say would be, "I may be right and you may be wrong" instead of, "I *am* right and you *are* wrong" then they would hardly ever have anything to fight about. It is a bizarre concept and would have made the writing of this book exceedingly tricky, but he certainly had a point.

Arlen died, after suffering several strokes, in 1999. Wilson said that his greatest ever achievement was his lifetime love affair with her, and that statement was later quoted in a beautiful 2003 proclamation by the Mayor of Santa Cruz, Emily Reilly, which declared 23rd July Robert Anton Wilson day.

Wilson himself died in 2007 at the age of 74. Despite his successes he rarely ever had any money, and health care during his last years was reliant on donations from fans. These donations were so generous as to leave him "...dumbfounded, flabbergasted, and totally stunned by the charity and compassion that has poured in here ...". Wilson's last message was written on his personal weblog explaining that the doctors had given him a few days to live. His final written words express the nature of the man perfectly:

> I look forward without dogmatic optimism but without dread. I love you all and I deeply implore you to keep the lasagna flying. Please pardon my levity, I don't see how to take death seriously. It seems absurd.

Wilson's legacy to the occult, mystical and politically radical subcultures of the English-speaking world is almost beyond measure, and still growing. His influence is (or perhaps "may be"!) particularly important in the fields of Chaos Magick, Transhumanism, Anarchism and joke religions. Joke religions are particularly important, for without humour there can be no love of life, and without love of life there can be no Dionysos.

Hail Eris! Praze "Bob"!

In 1964 a very, very odd book appeared in New Orleans. There were only five copies and its author was mysteriously known as Malaclypse the Younger, aided and abetted by his assistant Lord Omar Khayyam Ravenhurst III. In 1979 the book reappeared in a garish, eye-watering yellow cover. This was the fourth and most famous edition of *Principia Discordia or How I found Goddess And What I Did To Her When I Found Her*, the "Bible" of the Discordians.

According to the Discordian Catma (like a Dogma but more individualistic):

If you want in on the Discordian Society
then declare yourself what you wish
do what you like
and tell us about it
or
if you prefer
don't.
There are no rules anywhere.
The Goddess Prevails.

Principia Discordia is a book that tells you how to be a Discordian. It will not take long for the reader to realize how that, in itself, is a paradox. Effectively that is the whole point, and Discordianism in a nutshell.

Discordianism could simply be read as nothing more than a mickey-take of organised religion (which, indeed, it is) but that does the whole concept a disservice. In many ways the paradoxical and nonsensical nature of Discordianism can also be considered within the realms of Western Absurdist Zen, like the Rinzai Zen school of Japan which concentrates on paradoxical and impossible statements (*koans*) to break the students' linear-logical thought patterns. Personally, I consider it somewhat similar to the Taoism of Chuang Tzu (*aka* Zhuangzi). When Greg Hill/Malaclypse and Kerry Thornley/Lord Omar came up with the idea in a Californian bowling alley in 1958, they probably had no idea what they were spawning.

Discordianism can be summarised briefly as the worship of

Eris, the Goddess of Discord and Chaos and, frankly, a bit of a bitch. Paradoxically, as Thornley says in the introduction to the 1991 edition, "Organized religion preaches Order and Love but spawns Chaos and Fury. Why?" He then goes on to explain how order is imposed by our own minds and that the true reality is disorder and how the Discordian religion "works".

For instance, anyone or anything can be a Pope, or even a saint. You can lie in on Sundays and if you open up your pineal gland then you'll find Eris and She will solve all your problems, although She will also expect you to solve Hers in return. Discordianism also has its "rules" and principles such as *The Law of Fives* which was picked up and used quite effectively by Robert Anton Wilson; the basic doctrine of the *Pentabarf*; the *Aneristic Illusion* and the *Law of Eristic Escalation*, and symbols such as the *Golden Apple* and the *Sacred Chao* (pronounced "cow")[1].

Discordianism also has its own mythology beginning with the story of the *Judgement of Paris*, which incidentally goes on to cause the Trojan War. In the story Zeus does not invite Eris to the wedding of Peleus and Thetis because he considers her a troublemaker. This is known as *The Original Snub*, and in response Eris creates a golden apple with the word *Kallisti* ("to the prettiest") on it. All the Goddesses obviously think themselves the prettiest, so the Trojan prince Paris is brought in to judge, and Aphrodite is declared the winner due to her superior bribe of a sexy woman all of his own. The woman in question happens to be Helen, wife of Menelaus of Sparta, and thus begins the first major human war of Classical mythology.

Obviously, if the goddesses had not all been so shallow and vain then the whole business would have been easily sorted out and thousands of needless deaths would have been prevented. Eris, on the other hand, consoled herself by gatecrashing the party, chucking the apple in and enjoying a hot dog without a bun. In honour of this Discordians are required to partake of *No Hot Dog Buns*, except on Fridays when they are compulsory.

Another important part of Discordian mythology concerns the curse of the unsurprisingly Apollonian character, Greyface.

Greyface lived in 1166BC and taught that the universe is serious and orderly, and that to have fun is wrong. Discordians do not understand why his religion took off so well, especially in the face of such obvious evidence to the contrary, and have named his teachings *The Curse of Greyface*. As it says on page 00042 of the Principia:

> Greyface and his followers took the game of playing at
> life more seriously than they took life itself and were
> known even to destroy other living beings whose ways
> of life differed from their own.

To counteract the Curse of Greyface, Malaclypse the Younger and his Illuminated Adepts created the *Turkey Curse*. This is how you perform it:

> Take a foot stance as if you were John L. Sullivan
> preparing for fisticuffs. Face the particular grey-face you

wish to short-circuit, or towards the direction of the negative aneristic vibration that you wish to neutralize. Begin waving your arms in any elaborate manner and make motions with your hands as though you were Mandrake feeling up a sexy giantess. Chant, loudly and clearly:

GOBBLE, GOBBLE, GOBBLE, GOBBLE, GOBBLE!

The results will be instantly apparent.[2]

Does it work? Perhaps we should ask "Bob!"

The major difference between the Church of the Subgenius and Discordianism is that the Church of the Subgenius really is a church according to US law. A fully ordained Subgenius priest can, in many American states, legally perform weddings, baptisms, funerals and so on. Technically, this is done through a group in California called the Universal Life Church[3]. Ordination into the Church of the Subgenius costs (at present rates) $30 US, for which you receive full membership for life and several pamphlets, leaflets, certificates and so on. These detail how you can achieve "eternal salvation or triple your money back", and the nature of *The Conspiracy* and how the world may end tomorrow regardless of what day it is. Ordained Subgenius ministers include such luminaries as Robert Anton Wilson, Pee Wee Herman, David Byrne, Bruce Campbell and, of course, the author of this volume who goes by his official Subgenius title, *Revd. InsertNameHere.*

The Church has no god, but they do have a messiah. According to Subgenius legend the church was started some time in the 1950's by the world's greatest salesman, JR "Bob" Dobbs whose image appeared smoking a pipe on the back of comics hidden under the guise of advertisements asking, "Can you draw this?". He was working as a drilling equipment salesman when he had a vision of God (known as JHVH-1) on a home-built television. From this he wrote the Pre-Scriptures and encouraged the search for *Slack*. He has died and been reborn on several ocassions, most notably at his assassination in San Francisco in 1984.

The other legend of the beginning of the Church says that it sprang from a meeting of Doug Smith (Revd Ivan Stang) and Steve Wilcox (Dr Philo Drummond) in Dallas, Texas in 1979 – from which arose *Subgenius Pamphlet #1*, also known as *The World Ends Tomorrow and You MAY DIE!* Other friends joined in the fun and soon the Church of the Subgenius was born. The group passed on their literature to underground and cult figures and groups such as the band, Devo and the underground comic artist, Robert Crumb. They also made extensive use of the internet[4] as soon as it became available and have consequently grown massively throughout the world since. The legal entity known as the Subgenius Foundation now has its headquarters at Stang's house in Cleveland, Ohio. Obviously, nobody really believes this ludicrous version.

The church teaches that Subgenii are not real people (known as *pinks*) but are actually descended from Yetis. These *Yetisyn* will be rescued when the world ends on X-Day, 5th July 1998. There have been many excuses as to why that has not happened yet, such as the calendar being upside-down (thus giving the year 8661), that "Bob" has betrayed everybody and has run off with all their money, or that the calendar is clearly wrong and that the true year 1998 is still yet to occur. Nonetheless the X-Day camps, where Subgenii gather for the *Rupture* when the *X-ists* (Men from planet X) destroy the Earth and all the Yetisyn are taken away on the flying saucers of the alien Sex-Goddesses, are growing annually. This is how they describe themselves:

The Church Of The SubGenius is an order of Scoffers and Blasphemers, dedicated to Total Slack, delving into Mockery Science, Sadofuturistics, Megaphysics, Scatalography, Schizophreniatrics, Morealism, Sarcastrophy, Cynisacreligion, Apocolyptionomy, ESPectorationalism, Hypno-Pediatrics, Subliminalism, Satyriology, Disto-Utopianity, Sardonicology, Fascetiouism, Ridiculophagy, and Miscellatheistic Theology

It's very much a sign of their underground and subversive success that some right-wing elements in US law have, astonishingly, taken the Subgenius Foundation as a real and serious threat. In one ridiculous and much-publicised case a member had all contact with her young son denied to her by a particularly bigotted and humourless judge, on the grounds that her attendance at X-Day showed her to be "mentally ill and a pervert"[5]. Many of the Subgenius community donated money to help her fight her legal corner. The whole case, which took four years and wasted a lot of American taxpayers' money, is now over. She and her son are back together for good, but there still remains an astonishing and downright stupid court order preventing her from keeping Subgenius materials in her home.

The Church of the Subgenius should really be considered one of the most powerfully Dionysian groups in existence. Their effect on Apolline organisations such as the established church and the US Government, and their encouragement of underground experimental culture has been vast worldwide and is only getting larger. Yet all this has come from a parody religion which really does no more than take the mickey out of mindless orthodoxy, alien invasion cults and conspiracy theories.

The next section of this book is going to look forward, at people and groups who are taking the Dionysian spirit into the future and, perhaps, how we can do that ourselves. Before we move on, though, I wouldd like to take a moment to return to the Subgenius Foundation and consider their most famous mantra. It is a statement which, I personally feel, any Dionysian can truly live by:

Fuck 'em if they can't take a joke!

Dionysos Goes Forth

So far we have dealt with how Dionysos and the Dionysian Spirit have informed and enlivened society, especially in contrast to his Apolline opposite, but we have yet to look to the future.

Britain in the 21st century is a surprisingly Apolline place. We feel like we have more freedom and acceptance of individuality than ever before, yet we find ourselves with new and different restrictions and expectations of conformity. It was reported in several newspapers that the recent Labour government under Prime Minister Tony Blair enacted a new law on average every three hours. That is an astonishing and disturbing feat when you think about it.

It is also easy to see how the power of the advertising industry has never been stronger than it is now, and how consumerism has risen alarmingly in the last fifty years. The peer pressure on a school-age child, for instance, who does not have the latest mobile phone, hand-held computer or brand-name trainers, can be exceedingly traumatic.

Certain other social conventions are also just as strong as they have always been. The most obvious example of this is public nudity. Public nudity in England is not illegal[1] and has not been for quite some years, but should one walk nude into a public area one can almost guarantee immediate arrest. Such is the shock value of nudity that it is deliberately used in public protests as a means of getting noticed, most particularly by People for the Ethical Treatment of

Animals (PETA) and World Naked Bike Ride which, unlike PETA, really does have a nudist agenda.

How can the spirit of Dionysos continue to adapt, to shock and to break down the barriers to spirituality and individual freedom which are constantly being built in the modern West? In a world where Apollo needs Dionysos as much as Dionysos needs Apollo, who are the people who can carry that spirit forward and what can we do to help?

How can we do this? How can we experience ecstasy and enthusiasm for ourselves and spread that to the rest of society? Who are the New Dionysians?

Some Definitions

Definition in itself is an Apolline method and a Dionysian concept often defies simple definition, but it is still helpful to have an idea what is needed to carry the Spirit of Dionysos forward.

As we saw at the end of the first section, Dionysos is the god of life in all its fullness. He is the spirit of ecstasy (*ekstasis*) and enthusiasm (*entheos*). He is all about libertarian ideals, sensual and spiritual pleasures, powerful emotional depth and spontaneous joy. His is the realm of the heart rather than the mind, of spontaneity rather than organisation, of pluralism rather than unity.

A question arises that, should one wish to experience or promote the Dionysian spirit for oneself, is it really necessary to spend your life getting drunk or stoned? Are intoxicants the best answer?

The short answer is, of course, no. While this author has no wish to tell intelligent adults what they should or should not ingest, he is also definitely not going to encourage people to take potentially dangerous and often illegal substances, including alcohol. Such a choice is entirely up to the reader, but it should be noted that even the great Narco-Meister himself, William S Burroughs, is believed to have said that what can be done with drugs can be done in other ways.

What is really required to experience the Dionysian Spirit for oneself is the ability to "let go". The ideal is to put aside one's ego, repressions and inhibitions and temporarily lose oneself in the moment. That is easier said than done, of course, but when it is done well it creates a type of *ekstasis* whereby one stands outside one's "comfort zone" and allows *entheos* to happen in the form of enriching and powerful new experiences. Reports from first-time nudists reveal this pattern beautifully. When they finally, and very bravely, divest themselves of their last cloth barrier, they expect to feel vulnerable and exposed. Yet almost every single person describes the experience as "liberating", an extremely Dionysian word. Another superb and very effective way is through dancing.

Mad, Bad Dancing

I hereby declare that I want to encourage everyone to dance. It does not matter if you are good at it or not, how many uncoordinated left feet you have, or even how old or unhealthy you are. Everyone can dance in some way or another. I have seen profoundly deaf people and the wheelchair-bound dancing, and if they can do it, why not anybody? Nietzsche colourfully expounded the joys of dancing when he wrote in a letter to his sister, "I would believe only in a God that knows how to dance".

To be fair, we are not talking about ballet, the tango or the waltz, or even Morris dances and step dances. These are admirable and beautiful skills which undoubtedly bring immense pleasure to their exponents, but such rigorous learning is unnecessary for the Bacchante. Rather, the Dionysian dancer requires more freedom of expression and the chance to release their locked-up sense of playfulness and simply flow with the music, even if it looks clumsy or daft to people watching.

For this sort of exercise any music the listener likes will do the trick. Traditionally, the music of the Bacchanale consisted of drums and high reed-pipes (or similar), and there is indeed something remarkably primal about such a combination especially when played free-form by a group around a camp fire. The exact same, short-term effect can be got from almost any modern "rave". Dance music, which is designed specifically for that purpose will obviously be useful, but absolutely any music with a strong enough rhythm will work perfectly well if you let it. Personally, I love a good old Goth night.

The technique is simplicity itself. You dance! It requires a willingness to let go of one's inhibitions, hence the sale of alcohol in nightclubs, and not care that you may look foolish. That is the tricky part. The easy part is then to simply flow with the music and go. The result may simply be an endorphin rush, or it may be something deeper and more spiritual, but the experience will certainly be, as the nudists say, liberating.

On the subject of music, it may be worth considering whether there is specifically Dionysian music. Music *is* Dionysian, rather than Apolline, because of its dynamic and changing nature. Any live performance can only happen once and is, therefore, fleeting, momentary and subject to the emotions rather than rational experience.

Live music particularly, rather than its recorded counterpart, can be considered Dionysian, in much the same way as any other type of live performance. This is in comparison to the polished, manufactured and perfected results of recorded media which can be experienced again and again in much the same way as a painting or sculpture.

Unfortunately, there are also certain sorts of music which are cynically created to fit within specific parameters for the primary purpose of making money. Much "pop" music is of that nature, in that it is created to fit within certain expectations of what will sell to a specific demographic. There is definitely an art to creating a commercial pop song, and doubtless the musicians involved are rightly proud of their craft, but such music is almost shamefully Apolline in its nature. It is very much a modernised equivalent to Apollo stealing music from Pan.

More proudly Dionysian, though, are a great number of musicians who are doing it simply because it is what they love. Even if they are not much good at it there are still plenty of musicians and bands who defy categorisation and play the music that they really want to. Interestingly, these are often the ones who create what will sell by the boat-load a few years later. The Rolling Stones and the Doors were of this nature back in the 1960s, while the Sex Pistols in the 70s, the Smiths in the 80s and Nirvana in the 90s (among many others!) fulfilled the same roles.

The Triumph of Silliness

Dancing is a truly great way to experience the Dionysian Spirit for oneself, but there are other methods which can be used to promote and encourage the denting of Apolline expectations and repressions in one's larger society. One very effective method is to become involved in activities which could be described as "a bit silly", such as street theatre perhaps, or a flashmob.

By way of an example: A few months before writing this section I was required to attend a school performance. My second son, and all the other children in Year 6, were about to leave junior school and move up to their respective secondary schools. To celebrate this the school put on a performance which involved the singing of songs and children telling little stories of their memories from junior school. I really hate junior school shows like this because they are unconscionably dull, worthy and drab. Every child, regardless of talent or willingness, is expected to do *something* and the whole dreary situation has an air of inescapable, numbing duty. But, as a responsible father I was there to watch and support my son. Frankly, I could not find an excuse to avoid it!

As expected, it was dreadful. The songs, which were mostly about how "I can do anything if I really try", were sung as, "These are the words and this is how I've got to sing them" and the little speeches, with one or two notable exceptions, were almost all completely flat and expressionless. Then something very strange happened.

The next song was Starship's *Nothing's Gonna Stop Us Now*, which seemed an odd choice when one considers the lyric rather than just the title, and the children sang it pretty much as expected. In common with many rock songs, however, *Nothing's Gonna Stop Us Now* has a bridge. For any reader without a dictionary of musical terms, the bridge is (usually) an 8-bar break in a song roughly half or two-thirds of the way through, intended to stop the song becoming monotonous to the listener. The bridge in this particular song contains a guitar solo, which left the teachers with a problem: What do the kids do during the bridge? The answer was a stroke of genius: Get them all to play air guitar!

All of a sudden the stage was covered with manic 11 year-olds thrashing air guitars like miniature Hendrixes. It was controlled chaos, and a hilarious, ridiculous sight.

As soon as the bridge was over they all rushed back to their places and started singing again, *and they were magnificent*! They stood up straight, they were grinning, and they belted out the song like it mattered (and almost in tune). Suddenly they had stage presence and they were truly performing, and it lasted right to the end of the performance. It even survived the dull speeches of the headmaster.

So what has any of that got to do with Dionysos? Well, the point of the example is that something as small as eight bars of silliness managed to alter the whole performance. During the bridge the children were encouraged to let go, to free themselves in a safe way and simply be daft. This was their *ekstasis* which allowed the spirit of performance, the Dionysian Spirit, through. They achieved *entheos* through air guitar!

Those who like their silliness hardcore could always take a look at CIRCA, the Clandestine Insurgent Rebel Clown Army. The Rebel Clowns are actually quite a well-organised bunch whose aim is to make clowning dangerous and subversive again. To this end they appear at political protests to cause some small amount of mayhem in ridiculous and silly ways such as demanding that the President of the USA be replaced with a court jester for the Queen of England, and threatening actions with custard pies and buckets of whitewash if their demands are not heard.

Another recent clown action involved the infiltration of an anti-capitalist march. Half of the group dressed as a pro-capitalist group called Capitalism Represents Acceptable Policy, or CRAP for short. They marched through London carrying banners with such legends as *Tax the Poor*, *Bombs Not Bread* and *War is Good for the Economy*, and cheered companies with bad employee and union relations. They were eventually met by a large group of clowns who attacked them with tickling sticks and bad jokes, eventually chasing them from the area. As it says on their website, "A raging battle ensued and eventually the 'pro capitalists' were forced to flee in the face of the Clowns vision of an anti-capitalist utopia where everybody's nice to each other, money isn't everything and everyone wears colanders on their heads."[1]

Most adults really do not want to play air guitar in public or dress up as a clown, but there is a little gentle silliness we can all do to change the Apolline expectations of proper behaviour and add a bit of beautiful strangeness to the world while we do it. It is called the *Generosity Game*.

I recommend anyone who wants to try this to look it up on the internet[2] and hopefully find a few ideas. Put simply, since the 1950's and particularly the 70s and 80's the politics of Europe and America have increasingly been based on a concept called *Game Theory*. Boiled down to its essentials, Game Theory states that nobody ever does something for nothing. Even an act of altruism is performed in some way, according to Game Theory, for the benefit of the one performing it. The Generosity Game works with the intention of blowing that whole concept out of the water.

In the Generosity Game you give something away, or do something for somebody, anonymously and with absolutely no benefit to yourself. You might, for instance, buy something in a shop and instruct the shopkeeper to give it to the next customer. You might pay the entrance fee to an attraction for the next person to come along. You might send anonymous flowers or fruit to a stranger in hospital. The only limit here is your imagination.

Why on earth would you do this? Not for yourself, certainly, because the only thing you get out of it is a warm glow and a feeling of being a bit daft. In fact it costs you money, and you have absolutely no idea whether the next person will benefit or even if the shopkeeper will just eat the cake you bought himself. What you are doing is inserting a tiny bit of strangeness and beauty into someone else's life, and in doing so stepping outside the Apolline boundaries of "normal" behaviour. That which is not normal is, by definition, insane and the world needs a little insanity. Without it we would all go mad!

The Dark Side

In August 2011, Britain saw a short and unexpected spate of violent riots. Due to their opportunistic and entirely materialist nature they quickly became known as the first consumerist riots in British history, and they will certainly be debated for a long time to come. The riots had no specific political agenda, and no specific focal point. Rioters and looters who were interviewed had no particular reason for their actions except a nihilistic "fuck 'em" attitude. The country simply seemed to have gone mad.

The Russian critic and philosopher, Mikhail Bakhtin talked about the concept of the carnival[1] as a social release from the pressures of good behaviour. He was referring to the Mardi Gras, Saturnalia and the mediaeval Feast of Fools, events where the rules of normal behaviour no longer applied and people could release the pressure of their lives by acting in foolish and otherwise unacceptable ways. Bakhtin regarded the carnival as a basic human need. One of the many observations made of the August 2011 riots is that the people involved did not actually know why they were doing what they were doing. They simply cut loose and went temporarily insane.

I have said many times throughout this book that Dionysos and Apollo need each other. This is one of those examples. We no longer have a traditional carnival in the sense of the Feast of Fools or the Saturnalia, and have not had one for many years, which means that there is no safe release for the Dionysian energy in society. Thus it becomes sealed, bottled and builds up in pressure until some trigger causes it to explode in scenes of violence and destruction.

A similar example of the dark and destructive side of the Dionysian Spirit can be seen in the human sleep cycle. If normal waking life can be seen as Apolline, then dreams definitely belong to Dionysos. Experiments in sleep-deprivation have demonstrated that while we need sleep, what we really need are dreams.

A large body of evidence has been built up by Dr. William C. Dement[2] concerning the differences between, and the effects of, sleep and dream deprivation. It was found that waking subjects just as they entered a REM state had much the same effects as sleep deprivation in that concentration and judgement were all but destroyed and eventually subjects started to hallucinate. They began to dream while awake and became, effectively, insane.

There was one significant difference in that subjects woken from REM states and allowed to go back to sleep slipped back into dreams more and more quickly each time until it became practically impossible to prevent dreaming and the experiment had to be abandoned. It seems that we HAVE to dream.

It is pretty obvious from these examples that Dionysos has a frightening dark side which bursts out when repressed. Just like the Maenads tore apart Pentheus because he tried to prevent their rites, our society and even our own minds will do the same without a Bacchanale of their own. The Dionysian Spirit is more than just a part of us or of our society, it is an absolutely necessary part which will find expression whether we like it or not. It is up to us to make sure that expression is the right type.

Queers, Sluts and Sexy People

Apolline views are often at their strictest and most repressive where sexuality is concerned. Consequently, the radical campaigning push towards a more Dionysian viewpoint concerning the acceptance of sexual diversity is not only remarkably difficult, it is also vitally important. Interestingly, when breakthroughs are finally made by groups in the arena of human sexuality they are often extremely effective in the long term, despite the initial difficulty in achieving them. The Queer movement is one such important, possibly essential, group.

In the late 1960s the Stonewall riots in New York and Gay Pride in the UK managed to gain enough ground to make homosexuality legal, just. Homosexual sex was no longer punishable in England and Wales in 1967, as long as the two (and only two) partners were both over 21 and behind locked doors. In Scotland it was not legalised until 1980.

It was almost twenty years later before an openly gay song became a hit in the British music charts, *Small Town Boy* by Bronski

Beat (1984). The first gay kiss on primetime British Television did not happen until 1988, and consisted of a peck on the forehead between two Eastenders characters. Even today, when homosexuality is officially accepted and the age of consent is the same for both homo- and heterosexual relations[1], the sight of two men kissing outside of certain areas, like a gay club, still causes shock and consternation. This was particularly obvious when the British Broadcasting Corporation received a slew of complaints over a very mild, post-watershed, gay sex scene in its very popular BBC1 science fiction show, Torchwood.[2]

Things are much better now for gay people than they were 40 years ago, but they still have their problems, one of which is the Apolline tendency towards strict definitions of "acceptable" behaviour in gay and straight sexualities, and what is or is not "gay". This is where the Queer movement comes in.

The Queer movement works to expand acceptance both in and out of the gay community for those who do not fit the simple definition of homosexual. There is, for instance, a great deal of prejudice against bisexuals and pan-sexuals. There are also many issues concerning the social acceptance of asexuals, and of transgendered people, particularly those who wish to become or remain transgendered rather than change sex completely from one to another. Consequently there is now a growing Queer movement in the UK which is rejecting the modern image of the gay community (much of which, in Manchester at least, has become clichéd and taken over by corporate bodies for the purposes of financial profit) and recreating its own wider, more accepting, grass-roots community. They are small a small movement and have no money, but they have made the best use of modern technology by taking advantage of the ability to network and organise loudly and effectively on the internet through social media sites like Facebook, Twitter and MySpace.

Social media also gave many women the chance to be sluts, and proud of it! *Slutwalk* was a remarkable modern phenomenon which struck a loud and very obvious blow for women's rights and personal freedoms which all began with a stupid statement from an astonishingly thoughtless policeman.

On January 24th 2011 a Canadian police constable called Michael Sanguinetti was giving a talk on crime prevention in which he said, "Women should avoid dressing like sluts in order not to be victimized.".[3] Obviously many people were horrified at such an attitude, which laid the blame for rape directly on the victim, and decided to do something about it. Nine weeks later, on April 3rd over 3,000 people, mostly women and many of them deliberately dressed provocatively and carrying banners, gathered in Queens Park, Toronto and marched to the Toronto police headquarters.

Thus began the first Slutwalk, rescuing the word "slut" in an ironic manner and setting off the downhill roll of a global snowball. Since then, and mostly through the use of Facebook and Twitter, there have been Slutwalk events in major cities all over the world as far removed as San Francisco, Manchester UK, Delhi and Helsinki. At the time of writing they are still happening and being planned.

Opinion is divided as to the effectiveness of Slutwalk and its methods. Some say that women have the right to dress and choose what labels they wish without fear of rape and sexual harassment, citing the considerable amount of very convincing evidence that the connection between rape and state of dress is a media-fed myth. Others believe that the women involved are defining their sexuality in purely male and pejorative terms, which will be damaging for feminism in the long run. Either way though, Slutwalk caused a huge splash which will create ripples for a long time and all because people demand the right to be in control of their own sexuality (as, of course, they should) rather than be bound by Apolline social expectations.

The most important movement of sexual radicals is, paradoxically, one of the quietest. They have their meetings and their conventions, and they might even appear on television occasionally but mostly they just carry on with their lives as best they can and hope that the powers of social acceptability leave them alone. They are the polyamorists.

Polyamory is a word coined by the American Pagan priestess, Morning Glory Zell Ravenheart which simply means, in its mixed-up Greek-Latin fashion, "many loves". It is rumoured that the linguistically more correct terms, *multi-amory* and *polyphilia* were rejected on the grounds that one sounded like a mathematical operation and the other like a nasty disease!

Polyamory may be the ultimate Dionysian lifestyle because it completely defies definition in any but the loosest sense. The only thing polyamorists have in common is that they believe that it is perfectly possible and acceptable to love more than one partner at the same time. A polyamorist can be single, married, gay, straight, bisexual, kinky, "vanilla", promiscuous, or even a virgin. There are exclusive triads, amorphous multi-partner groupings, couples with a bit extra, partners of partners and metamours, and even friends-with-benefits.

The most important quality required of, and generally common to, the polyamorist is probably one of the most difficult for most people in modern Western society to accept or understand. It is the sense of *compersion*, or as it is sometimes called in Britain, "feeling frubbly"[4]. Compersion means to take pleasure in somebody else's pleasure, particularly in seeing one's partner enjoying a different partner. This is not a sexual thrill, although the sexual element is not precluded. It is rather a kind of *love-plus*, whereby what makes one happy is the fact that someone you love is happy. Compersion is a very giving kind of love, and we are simply not brought up to feel like that.

Our view of marriage and relationships in the modern West is one of the most Apolline areas of our lives. We have a brainwashed, "drummed-in" social expectation of monogamy as the *only* type of adult sexual love. We are taught to have one partner at a time, and one partner only, and that the partner is somehow "ours" as if they are property. To have another partner is considered by the outside world to be "cheating", regardless of the intimate arrangements of the people involved. Monogamy, or at least mono-amory, is the default expectation of our love songs, of our films and soap operas and is enshrined in our marital laws. There are even those who, ignoring the considerable and ever-increasing evidence to the contrary, consider monogamy "natural" to the human species.

The polyamorist says that is not the case. There are no rules except the ones we impose on ourselves and each other. If you can love both parents, and all three of your children, then why can you not love two or more sexual partners? Why must a child be brought up by one or two parents? Why not three? Why not a communal group where all the children are brought up by all the adults and all the adults love each other? Who, in the final analysis, has the right to decide what is and is not true love?

The beautifully Dionysian polyamorous movement has been growing for quite some time and its quiet popularity is evidence by the growth of polyamorous films and literature. One of the earliest of these books is Robert Heinlein's *Stranger in a Strange Land*, which was a major influence on Morning Glory Zell Ravenheart who, with her partner Otter/Oberon, founded the Church of All Worlds[5] in California, based directly on the fictitious organisation described by Heinlein.

The "bible" of Polyamory is, of course, *The Ethical Slut* by Dossie Easton and Catherine Liszt. Other works are also coming to the fore, such as the highly recommended anthropological study of human sexuality, *Sex at Dawn* by Christopher Ryan and Cacilda Jethá, which looks closely at how "natural" (or not!) our societies' expectations of monogamy really are. Polyamorous themes in film are also appearing more and more often, in such movies as *Rita, Sue and Bob Too*, *The Hunger* and Spike Lee's *She's Gotta Have It*.[6]

The Dionysian Underground

In the sub-culture of Occultism there have always been individuals whose dearest wish is to further the aims of human spiritual freedom and liberty, very often by attempting to live the life they would wish to promote. We can consider them extremists, perhaps, but their lives are changing the boundaries and accepted norms of magickal practice and making new methods of ekstasis and entheos available to the spiritual seeker. Such people can be considered part of an underground movement within the Dionysian paradigm, whether they deal with Dionysos in a conscious fashion or not. One such remarkable extremist is Genesis Breyer P. Orridge.

Genesis can be considered a truly self-made person. Out of respect for Genesis' personal preference, and for reasons which will become clear, I am going to refer to Genesis using the pronoun, *they*. I beg the reader's indulgence for a little while and apologise for the almost inevitable confusion that is about to be caused.

Genesis was born a male called Neil Megson in south Manchester in 1950, was raised mostly in Loughton, Essex and went to Hull University in 1968. They became interested in the Occult and dropped out of university, firstly by joining a commune in London in 1969 and later by creating a "prankster collective" in Hull. The collective swiftly transformed into a performance art group which was known as *COUM Transmissions*. The group was heavily influenced by William

Burroughs and Brion Gysin, and their work included a strong tendency to focus on sexual taboos. COUM was controversial enough to cause something of a stir in what one would expect to have been a thoroughly jaded area, the art world of 1970s Britain. The 1976 *Prostitution* exhibition led to a debate in parliament about the uses of public funding, and Genesis was labelled by the press as a "wrecker of civilisation". Apart from Genesis and two other members, namely the erotic model and musician, Cosey Fanni Tutti and the musician and designer, Peter "Sleazy" Christopherson, the membership of COUM was very fluid and unsurprisingly, the project eventually folded. The three permanent members went on to form a radical new band, *Throbbing Gristle*, with a fourth member, Chris Carter. In many ways Throbbing Gristle carried on where COUM left off, with deliberately disturbing performances intended to explore the darker side of humanity rather than just make pretty and commercial music. They did this by using loud and distorted sound samples and tape loops, along with images lifted from pornography and pictures from Nazi death camps, over which Genesis or Cosey would perform spoken-word pieces. They were quickly adopted by the British Punk movement. The last Throbbing Gristle performance was in 1981 when the band was closed down and Genesis started their new project, the extremely influential Psychick TV. Psychick TV continued in a variety of guises, including Thee Temple ov Psychick Youth and PTV3 (and despite an appalling personal tragedy) until 2009 when Genesis announced their retirement to concentrate on art and poetry.

There were two great loves in Genesis' life. The first was their first wife, Paula P. Orridge (Alaura O'Dell), who was the mother of their two daughters. They divorced in 1981. The second was Lady Jaye Breyer P. Orridge (Jacqueline Mary Breyer), whom they married in 1993. Genesis and Lady Jaye realised that they were not two people but one person in two bodies, a *pandrogyne* (hence the pronoun), a person they labelled Breyer P. Orridge. They undertook courses of plastic surgery, including breast implants, to look as identical as possible. Lady Jaye said in an interview, "We view Breyer P. Orridge as a separate person who is both of us" The appalling tragedy mentioned above happened in 2007 when Lady Jaye died suddenly of a heart attack thought to have been brought on by her long-term battle with stomach cancer. She was 38 years old. At present, Genesis has carried on the pandrogeny project via a Breyer P Orridge website[1] which displays their new artwork.Genesis has been an exceptionally influential person, musically in being a leading light in the development of both punk and acid-house music and in pushing the borders of performance art, but particularly in the questioning of identity and sexuality and what it means to be a "person". Breyer P. Orridge was a separate person made of two people who were both the same person. Such a statement is beyond easy and simplistic concepts of gender, and the ability of our language to cope with it.

Hakim Bey is less complex than Genesis, but nonetheless interesting and influential in the modern Occult movement. Also known as the Goofy Sufi or, more prosaically, as Peter Lamborn Wilson, Bey has been writing as an anarchist and spiritual libertarian since the 1970s. His books range around such diverse topics as Persian picture rugs, Charles Fourier, Chuang Tzu and environmentalism for the Hermeticist, but his book[2], *T.A.Z.: The Temporary Autonomous Zone, Ontological Anarchy, Poetic Terrorism* explains the concepts for which he is best known.

A TAZ is a temporary space, such as an event like a party or rave, where the normal rules of society are suspended. The ideal is to create a state for everybody where the mind is freed from imposed controlling mechanisms so that the real natures of, and relationships between, people can emerge. Many who assume that human beings are inherently selfish would consider this a bad idea but the relative success of rave culture, the Cacophony Society's development of the Burning Man Festival and even the 60' *Love-In* seem to belie any worries. *Ontological Anarchy* is very much the mind-set need for a TAZ, in that it is no mind-set at all because it regards definite views and ideas as baseless. *Poetic Terrorism* is the act of creating the TAZ and possibly a little Ontological Anarchy in the minds of witness, through art and other "criminal acts".

Unfortunately, due to his sexual poetry and tastes, Bey has been accused by some in the Occult subculture of paedophilia, or at least being an apologist for paedophilia. While personally I would not like to make a judgement either way, it does appear to be based on his taste for homosexual love poetry rather than any evidence of paedophile activity. He has certainly never been arrested or charged in a court of law for any such behaviour, but in the climate of the early 21st century it is a stain that is hard to remove. Perhaps judgement should be reserved, in favour of Bey's writings and radical thought and his love of the irrational which, as was shown by the Dadaists, the Surrealists and the Situationists, to bring about new ways of looking at the world and the breaking down of ossified thought patterns. Here is a quote from his essay, Poetic Terrorism:

> Kidnap someone & make them happy ... Organize a
> strike in your school or workplace on the grounds that it
> does not satisfy your need for indolence & spiritual
> beauty ... Dress up. Leave a false name. Be legendary.
> The best PT is against the law, but don't get caught. Art
> as crime; crime as art.

An Australian by birth but now truly international, Orryelle Defenestrate Bascule does not have an easy name to understand and, as such, it matches its owner perfectly. I will leave the readers to work out for themselves what, if anything, it means to them.

One should really do the same with Orryelle's work which has qualities both beautiful and fascinating, and at the same time disquieting and confusing. S/He calls what s/he does *Performancy*, and that is as good a name as any for hir complex mixture of theatre, music, art, written work and ritual which s/he and a troupe of friends take around the world. These performances often include body modifications such as piercing and tattooing as part of the activity as well as the more usual dance, music, spoken word and physical theatre.

As an artist on canvas Oryelle can very much be considered a natural successor to such remarkable occult artists as Austin Osman

Spare and Rosaleen Norton. S/He also edits and produces an occult publication called *Si/KMi/K MagiZain* full of articles and art of some of the most cutting-edge work in occult circles. Issues also contain a DVD and CD to add performance to the written and painted work.[3]

The Dionysian Underground is also a lot more than just a concept of an undercurrent in society. There really is a Dionysian Underground, a non-organised organisation which was created by the historian /philosopher known mysteriously as Kaotec XXIII, and four (some say six) friends in London in 1997. The basic premise was to create a non-hierarchical group with the purpose of spreading the Dionysian current throughout society thus championing liberty, free communalism and self-realisation.

Although less physically active as a specific group nowadays the Dionysian Underground was instrumental in certain social and political actions during the early years of the 21st century. These included a psychedelic party for Dionysos' birthday, an attempt to reclaim Eros from Piccadilly Circus during a May Day demonstration and involvement with one of Orryelle's Metamorphic Ritual theatre productions. That particular production also included a performance by the sexually fascinating, but now sadly defunct, Pagan rock band, Rockbitch. They also offer support to other radical libertarian movements such as the Sexual Freedom Coalition and the pro-Cannabis lobby.

The Dionysian Underground, though, is an unstructured movement and has been subject to the criticism that it does not actually exist. This is perfectly understandable when you consider that there are no official memberships, no clubhouse and no rules. Having said all that, the presence of the Dionysian Underground working through the internet and social networking media is spreading like an untended grapevine[4]. On one of their websites, of which there are several, they describe themselves as *an informal network of like minded adepts working within the Dionysian Current*. Therefore, within the Dionysian Underground it is considered that self-declaration can make one a member of the Dionysian Underground by virtue of the fact that one is working within the Dionysian current. Orryelle has been jokingly described as the founder member of the Dionysian Down-Underground and I have founded my own personal branch, the Dionysian Metrolink Light Transport System (because we don't have an Underground here in Manchester!).

Joking aside, the Dionysian Underground is an important movement, particularly through its members' use of the internet and social networking to promote the Dionysian paradigm. They lend their support, both as a group and individually, to libertarian social and political movements and the pushing forward of occult thought in general.

The New Dionysians

We have come almost to the end of the book now, but there is one more question left to ask: "Who are the New Dionysians?". We have looked at the Dionysian current and those who have carried it, from Ancient Greece right up to the present day and in every corner of the world. Who, though, will carry that current forward in the future?

The answer, I believe, lies with the *Pagans*.

Technically known as neo-Pagans, the modern Pagan movement has been growing and evolving publicly since the 1950's. Pagans did exist before the 1950's but it was primarily the occult revivals of the late 1960s and mid 1980s which brought the movement to the fore and increased its exposure and popularity. We owe a debt of gratitude to the funding fathers of modern Wicca, Gerald Gardner and Alex Sanders for that.

The adherents of Paganism are a loose conglomeration of many "paths" from the very popular and well known philosophies of Wicca, Druidry and Heathenism, right through to individual shamanisms, Chaos Magick and simple all-round spirituality. "Pagan" is a term so wide-ranging it is almost impossible to properly define, yet at the same time it is by far the fastest growing religion in the whole Western world.

There are some Pagans, of course, who are definitely Apolline. These would be the strict Reconstructionists who are attempting to recreate, as nearly as possible in the modern world, the ancient religions to which they feel an affinity. The most popular of the Reconstructionists religions are those with extant writings such as the Nordic or Hellenic Greek beliefs. I have no wish to criticise the Reconstructionists and, in fact, have a great deal of respect for their learning and devotion to an ideal, I simply would not call them Dionysian.

The ones I would call Dionysian are the plain, ordinary Pagans: the generalists, the Jacks-of-All-Trades, the "floating voters". Whether they know it or not, these are the people who are pushing Paganism forward into new and interesting realms, simply because they do not follow a specific path but are willing to appropriate bits and pieces from other paths and put them together in experimental ways. These are also the ones trying out new ideas and methods based on principles they have learned rather than following instructions to the letter.

All across the world there are modern Pagans attempting to find spirituality on their own terms. These are the ones you bump into at conferences who, when asked their path reply with statements like, "Errrm, well I don't really have one, exactly. It's more sort of …" They are the people searching for and experiencing ekstasis and entheos in new and exciting ways, defying those who say, *"You can't do that!"*, and they are having a lot of fun doing it too

The book will finish with a poem on the following page, but before that there is one request I would like to make of my fellow modern Dionysians. I would like us all to look at the following quotation from the remarkable Dionysian historian/philosopher, Steve Ash and consider it. Perhaps take it to heart, maybe even consider it the nearest thing the modern Dionysian movement has to a commandment:

"Our task is to re-enchant the world and make it magickal again"

The following poem was written by the urban shaman and poet, John Constable (aka John Crow) in honour of the Dionysian Underground. It seems a fitting end-piece to bring us right up-to-date with the Dionysian Spirit.

THE DIONYSIANS

Let's go Pan

Let's go pagan

Let's wake up Her Majesty with Michael Fagan

Let's reinvent the art of the urban shaman

Throw a wild party in the wrecked heart of Babylon

Let's make a magic potion

Let's brew it in a cauldron

Re-awake the snake

Make poetry in motion

Let's go night tripping skinny dipping in the ocean

Let's go pink

Let's go punk

Let's smile for the camera with a mouth full of spunk

Let's shadow-box with angels until we punch-drunk

Let's get feathered

Let's get furred

Let's shake a hoof with the horny goat-herd

Let's raise the roof and then let fly the bird

Let's go Pan

Let's go primal

Let's do the Old God Man Shamanic Revival

Catch as catch can and scratch-scratch it on vinyl

Let's go Trickster

Let's go Tantra

Let's bang a gong and sing a Bagavati Mantra
Paint our bodies red and blue create a living Yantra
Let's advance
Let's retreat
Let's trance dance to a tribal break beat
Let's Do It All Night
Let's stir up and shake up
Let's give ourselves a fright when we take off our
make-up
Love-bite the Sleepers until they finally
Wake up!

John Constable >
< Crow to the Dionysian Underground

Notes

The Myths of Dionysos

Ancient Greece

1. Information taken from Hump Jones, "300, the hottest gay porno of all time", by Justin Boland. http://www.humpjones.com/rear/entry/300_the_hottest_gay_porno_of_all_time/

The Birth of Dionysos

1. Some readers may find the use of the present tense disconcerting. I have written this way because I consider mythology to be timeless. In other words, happening at all times and in all places at once rather than at a specific time in a specific place.

Dionysos' Childhood

1. Robert Graves, "The Greek Myths"
2. ibid

Early Life

1. This is in common with a great many mythological characters similar to Dionysos, such as Achilles, King Arthur or Jesus. The mysterious or hidden childhood appears to be a normal part of the archetype
2. Literally meaning a band or company, usually of followers or worshippers.

The Bacchae

1. Available as an online text at http://beauty.gmu.edu/AVT472/
AVT472%20Paula/Euripides%20The%20Bacchae%20%28e-
text%29.pdf

Love and Sex

1. According to Lou Hart, co-creator of Queer Pagan Camp.
2. This story is not told in full by any of the usual sources of Greek
mythological tales, though several of them hint at it. It is recon-
structed on the basis of statements by Christian authors; these have
to be treated with reserve because their aim is to discredit pagan
mythology: http://en.wikipedia.org/wiki/Prosymnus

Behind the Myths

1. Michael Grant, "Myths of the Greeks and Romans"
2. ibid.
3. Plato, "The Republic" 398d-399c
4. Genesis 32:24-32 and
   Robert Graves "The White Goddess"
5. ibid.
6. The Mabinogion, "Hanes Taliesin" (The Book of Taliesin)
7. James Frazer and Robert Graves particularly.
8. RJ Stewart, "The Mystic Life of Merlin"

Dionysos to Jesus via Orpheus

1. Robert Graves, "The White Goddess"

2. Bertrand Russell, "History of Western Philosophy"
3. ibid
4. Robert Graves, "The White Goddess"
5. Exodus 23:19
6. Bertrand Russell, "History of Western Philosophy"
7. Martin A Larson, "The Essene-Christian Faith"
8. Matthew 26:26-28

Dionysian Heroes

Early Days

1. Sex was especially controlled in the mediaeval church. St Augustine considered sex only for breeding and a hideous evil. *"Shameful lust, however, could not excite our members, except at our own will, if it were not a disease"* On Concupiscence, Book II, chap. 55

The Renaissance and Onwards

1. Translation by J.M. Cohen, 1955. Gargantua, Ch.54.

Romance

1. The Libertine, 2004. Directed by Laurence Dunmore. Cert 18.
2. Robinson's "Beaux and Belles of England" can be downloaded for free from the Project Gutenberg website. http://www.gutenberg.org/ebooks/9822
3. There is a statue of Byron in Athens. There is also a street named in his honour and, more recently, a hotel.

America

1. Reynolds, David S., "Walt Whitman's America: A Cultural Biography."

Germany

1. Published in 1918
2. Nobody knows what Nietzsche's illness was and many theories have been proposed including syphilis, vascular dementia, manic depression and CADASIL syndrome (which is a hereditary stroke disorder).
3. Published in 1872, when he was 27 years old.

Turning the Century

1. The book eventually passed the new 1959 Obscene Publications Act on the grounds of its literary merit, but not before the chief prosecutor, Mervyn Griffith-Jones made a complete fool of himself by asking if it was something "you would wish your wife or servants to read"
2. Oscar Wilde, 16th October 1854 to 30th November 1900
3. The International Otto Gross society is dedicated to preserving his work. Their website can be found at http://www.ottogross.org/

Divine Decadence, Darling!

1. John Kenrick, "A History of Cabaret"
2. André Breton, "Surrealist Manifesto" 1924
3. Dita von Teese, "Burlesque and the Art of the Teese"

4. "… he, like other magicians, carried inside him the seed of his own downfall. The self-centred child who disliked his mother … had almost no capacity for natural affection" Colin Wilson, "The Occult" 1971.

Post-War 20th Century

1. I believe the Irish for *Language of the Water* would be *Teanga na hUisce*. (Please feel free to correct me.)
2. Jack Kerouac, "On the Road" 1955 (various places in the text)
3. Jack Kerouac, "The Dharma Bums" 1958

Dionysos Around the World

India

1. Gavin Flood, "An Introduction to Hinduism" 1996
2. "The Kapalika branch of Shaivism may also have its origins in the Veda. The Kapalikas are also called Soma-Siddhantins, as their practices are thought to be connected with the Soma ritual" from http://shivadarshana.blogspot.com/2007/05/tradition-of-shiva.html

China

1. Tao Te Ching. Trans. Stephen Addis and Stanley Lombardo 1993
2. As described by Daniel Reid in the introduction to "The Tao of Helth, Sex and Longevity" 1989

Africa

1. The Nok, http://www.mrdowling.com/609-testr.htm

2. ibid.

3. ibid.

4. http://en.wikipedia.org/wiki/Ethiopia

Judaism

1. Jeremiah 7:18

The Arabic-Islamic World

1. "Believers, wine and games of chance, idols and divining arrows are abominations devised by Satan. Avoid them so that you may prosper." The Quran, surah 5:90

2. Edward Fitzgerald (1809-1883). The *Rubáiyat* is still popular and available in a version with beautiful Art Nouveau-style illustrations by René Bull.

3. RA Wilson, "The Illuminati Papers" 1976

Dionysos Across The Millenium

Ken Kesey

1. Known as Project MKULTRA, which extentend from 1950 until the early 60s studying mind alteration and control. A report was released in 1977 and a .pdf copy is held by the New York Times here http://www.nytimes.com/packages/pdf/national/13inmate_ProjectMKULTRA.pdf

2. Including the joke canonisation of Timothy Leary at a festival in 1978.

Timothy Leary

1. Timothy Leary, "High Priest" 1995
2. Known as the Concord Prison Experiment.

Dead Pop Stars

1. There is a rather bizarre little group known as the *27 Forever* club which includes amongst its members Robert Johnson, Kurt Cobain and Amy Winehouse, as well as our four heroes.
2. For stealing cars. In May 1961 Hendrix was given the choice of enlisting or spending two years in jail.
3. Laurie Jacobson, "Hollywood Heartbreak" 1984.
4. The theories are considered with clarity and balance in "No One Here Gets Out Alive" (1980) by Jerry Hopkmins and Danny Sugarman

New York in Velvet

1. Apparently Solanas was angry at Warhol after he had lost a script she had given him and turned her away from The Factory.
The Rise, Fall and Rise of Nico.
1. The photographer was Herbert Tobias and Nico was the nickname of the film maker, Nikos Papatakis
2. Last heard of living in France and a photographer and actor in his own right, using the stage name, Ari Boulogne
3. The stage play, "Nico Icon" by Stella Grundy chronicles the period that Nico spent living in a squat in Salford and battling heroin addiction. On a personal note, I was in my early twenties at that

time and it is a small fantasy that maybe, just maybe, I once unknowingly shared a bus ride with the great Nico.

RAW

1. The whole incident was recorded at the time and became the culmination of the Rolling Stones documentary film "Gimme Shelter" (1970). The question remains as to why Hunter took a gun to a concert in the first place, and many of the witnesses were convinced that he was attempting to harm Mick Jagger.

2. Published in "The Illuminati Papers" 1980

Hail Eris! Praze "Bob"!

1. It is recommended that the reader looks up these concepts for themselves because a proper explanation would take up the rest of the book!

2. From Principia Discordia. It is probably best just to get your own copy. I can't promise that it will make any more sense, but it might help.

3. Any reader who wishes to become a minister of the Universal Life Church may do so instantly and for free via the internet at http://www.themonastery.org/

4. http://www.subgenius.com/

5. Judge James P Punch, Orleans County Court, New York. Punch is a devout Catholic who recused (ie disqualified) himself from the case when this and his other questions and statements hit the internet.

Dionysos Goes Forth

1. "Indecent Exposure" does not exist in England and Wales. The use of nudity to "harass, alarm or distress" is covered by the Public Order Act 1986. in other words, public nudity is perfectly legal unless it bothers somebody.

The Triumph of Silliness
1. http://www.clownarmy.org/operations/crap.html
2. http://www.facebook.com/group.php?gid=58964688082

The Dark Side
1. Mikhail Bakhtin, "Rabelais and his World", a dissertation written during the Second World War but not published until 1965.
2. At the time of writing, Dr Dement is still working (at the age of 83) as the Professor of Psychiatry and Behavioural Science as Stanford University School of Medicine, Stanford, California. He teaches an extremely popular course called, "Sleep and Dreams"

Queers, Sluts and Sexy People
1. The Sexual Offences (Amendments) Act 2000.
2. Series 4, "Miracle Day". Episode 7, "Immortal Sins". UK broadcast 25th August 2011.
3. At Osgoode Hall Law School, York University, Toronto. Sanguinetti has since made written apology.
4. Although, in my own involvement with the polyamorous community I have never yet heard anyone use the word, "Frubbly" I

think they would find it embarrassing.

5. Anyone wishing to research the Church of All Worlds will find their website a useful and informative place to start http://www.caw.org/

6. "Rita, Sue and Bob Too", Alan Clarke 1987. "The Hunger", Tony Scott 1983. "She's Gotta Have It", Spike Lee 1986.

The Dionysian Underground

1. http://www.invisible-exports.com/artists/genesisporridge/breyerporridge.html

2. Published in 1985 and 1991 although Bey has made it freely available on the internet for pirate copies to be made http://hermetic.com/bey/taz_cont.html

3. Oryelle's "Mutation Parlour" is possibly the weirdest website you could ever see http://www.crossroads.wild.net.au/index.html

4. The Dionysian Underground are literally all over the internet. I suggest that the reader simply types "Dionysian Underground" into a search engine and peruses whatever comes up. There will be plenty.

Lightning Source UK Ltd.
Milton Keynes UK
UKOW06f2234130515

251491UK00001B/6/P